NINE BASIC MODULES OF CHRISTIAN HEALING
THE TEACHING MANUAL

NINE BASIC MODULES
of
CHRISTIAN HEALING

THE TEACHING MANUAL

Compiled and expanded by

Randolph Vickers

from original material written by
Dorothy, Karen, David & Randolph Vickers

Published in Great Britain by
The Northumbrian Centre of Prayer for Christian Healing
Beggars Roost, 26 Painshawfield Road, Stocksfield, Northumberland NE43 7PF

The right of Randolph Vickers to be identified as author of this work
has been asserted by him in accordance with the
Copyright, Design and Patents Act 1988

Cover design by Roger Judd

ISBN 978-0-9555353-0-7

Printed in Great Britain
by Bookmarque Ltd, Croydon

Contents

THE CONTRIBUTORS

Following requests from churches and groups in a number of countries, this book was compiled from original material written by David Vickers BA (Hons) Theology, Leeds; Karen Vickers, BA, Dip A.Th; Dorothy Vickers, Dip. Ed., Dip Psychodynamic Counselling, WPF; Randolph Vickers, MA Applied Theology, Newcastle.

The Directors also pay tribute to the contribution to the success of the teaching modules played by the other members of the team at the Centre, who bring knowledge and skills from other relevant disciplines.

INTRODUCTION

He sent them to preach the kingdom and to heal the sick
                                                    Luke 4:2

The Northumbrian Centre of Prayer for Christian Healing prepared a teaching programme of nine basic modules.

The course is designed for all those interested in learning the basics about Jesus' ministry of healing. Part of the vision for the Centre is to equip the saints for the work of ministry in the area of healing. We have identified nine key areas, which we see as basic modules for everyone involved in the healing ministry. Each one is written as a separate, stand-alone module and together they build into a basic programme. And we stress that this is a basic programme. As our vision in teaching these courses is about equipping the saints for ministry (not just teaching on it), these two and a half hour sessions should include elements of appraisal and activitation.

This teaching manual is based on these modules and is suitable for use by leaders to train Christians in this ministry and as a reference handbook for those who have been through the training. Although each of the modules is written so that they can stand alone and can therefore be accessed in any order, they all stand on the premise taught in the first module — 'that it is the nature and will of God to heal'. Anyone who is going to be involved in Jesus' ministry of healing must know and be certain of this, right deep down in their innermost being. Therefore, if it at all possible, I would urge that every endeavour is made to ensure that every delegate is firmly rooted in this understanding before tackling the other sessions.

The modules are numbered in the order that we first wrote them but this is not necessarily the best order for teaching. My preferred order for study would be:

(1) The Nature and Will of God to Heal (3) Know Your Authority in Jesus (4) Gifts of the Spirit (2) Listening to Others. (8) Listening to God (5) The Cycle of Grace (7) Be Clear for Prayer (8) Models of Ministry (9) Healing through Worship.

The material in the chapters should be taught in relation to and in the order presented by the handout material given as an appendix for each module. Anyone teaching the modules is free to reproduce the handout material for distribution to those attending the sessions but we would ask that the logo for the Northumbrian Centre of Prayer for Christian Healing is always used.

The style of the material can be quite different from module to module because although I, Randolph Vickers, have brought it all together Dorothy and David originally wrote a number of the modules. Audio recordings of the initial presentation of most of the sessions are available.

Chapter 10 is a series of training wheel prayers for the situations most commonly encountered.

All the teaching is based on Scripture. At the time of writing this book Randy, Dorothy, David and Karen had over one hundred years of combined experience of working in this area of Jesus' ministry. Therefore the teaching whilst built on Scripture, embodies personal revelation, learned knowledge from others, experience, testimony and straightforward pragmatism.

This teaching is basic to the equipping of the saints to work in this ministry but is by no means the sum total. The Northumbrian Centre expands this teaching for the committed through further, longer seminars. Also Randolph's book *The Anointing to Heal* is essential reading for all involved in this ministry.

For churches or groups who are interested, teams from the Centre can be available to come out to them and teach the material. This will entail a commitment of one week for the delegates. Certification of attendance is available. Given committed leadership there is the possibility of being authenticated as an Extension Centre of the Northumbrian Centre of Prayer for Christian Healing. This will involve ongoing training and supervision from the Centre.

Those teaching are encouraged to use their own anecdotes, case studies, testimonies, etc., where applicable, in place of those given in the manual.

Other courses available through the Centre:
- Defeating our Inner Strongholds. (This as usually held through a weekend Fri/Sun.)
- Listening to God and Speaking out. (This is a basic introduction to prophecy and involves one evening and a full day – usually Friday evening and all day Saturday.)
- Models of Ministry expanded. (This is a full day.)
- Creativity and Healing in Worship. (This is a full day.)
- Creativity Retreat. (This is a full day.)
- The Powerful Role of Praise & Worship in the Christian's life. (This involves two evening sessions and a full day.)
- Going Deeper in Arts and Worship. (This is a full day.)
- Introduction to how to study the Bible (3 sessions).
- How to study the Bible —going deeper (at least 3 sessions).

- Quiet Days. (A number of these days are run throughout the year.)
- Annual Conference. (Each year we have a residential weekend conference, which is led by an acclaimed speaker, invited from outside our own organisation.)

MODULE 1

THE NATURE AND WILL OF GOD TO HEAL

• *During the session the delegates should be encouraged to give their understandings of the various sections before giving them the references to look up.*
• *Ask the delegates whether or not they agree with the proposition that it is the nature and will of God to heal.*
• *Let them voice their arguments pro and con for a few minutes, then lead into recounting the following account of the time of the Passover.*

Have you ever noticed what is probably one of the biggest healing events recorded in the Scriptures? I think that even if we had no further evidence than Exodus chapter 15 we could see that God's will for his people is that when they follow his word they will all be healed. The Hebrews had been treated as slaves for generations. A life in slavery was hard, and the Egyptians made the lives of the Jews bitter with hard work. We know from Exodus 12:37 and Numbers 11:21 that 600,000 men, as well as women and children, left Egypt on the night of the Passover. Various commentators suggest that this could mean somewhere between 1.5 million and 3 million people in total may have been involved. Had they enjoyed full modern medical care and a wholesome diet, in a population of that size we may well imagine that there there would have been many among them who were sick. I have no doubt that, in the hours before the angel of death passed over the houses with the blood of sacrifice painted on the door posts, there would have been some sick, fragile and lame. In fact we know from Scripture that there was sickness amongst them because in Deuteronomy 7:15 it says, *The Lord will keep you free from every disease. He will not inflict on you the horrible diseases you knew in Egypt, but he will inflict them on all who hate you.*

Yet, referring to the Hebrew people God brought out from Egypt, Psalm 105:37 tells us that among the tribes brought out by God there was nobody who was 'feeble'. This is made especially clear in the AV and NKJV translations of the Bible. (NIV has: no-one faltered.) It would have been extremely surprising if, in that large population, there had been no frail people at all, no-one whose physical condition was such that they might have faltered, and in the natural we might think that would be impossible, but with God all things are possible. That the fact that none were 'feeble' is included in the scriptural account signals that something significant had happened. Then because of their disobedience when they did not obey God, all but three were to die during the forty years in the wilderness. Yet remember that it is also remarkable that, as we read in Deuteronomy 8:4, their clothes did not wear out and their feet did not swell during these forty years. I deduce that, at the great Exodus from Egypt, when God delivered his people from slavery, he healed all who were sick in that one night. And can you imagine all those old women walking through the hot desert for so long —and not even one swollen ankle, no sore feet and blistered feet? Does that not tell us something about a God whose nature and will is for his people to be well?

The biblical expression *Jehovah Rapha,* the Lord who heals, is of great significance here. *"If you listen carefully to the voice of the LORD your God and do what is right in his eyes, if you pay attention to his commands and keep all his decrees, I will not bring on you any of the diseases I brought on the Egyptians, for I am the LORD, who heals you"* (Exodus 15:26). The word rapha literally means 'to heal'.

• *Have the definitions on an overhead. Discuss the meaning of the words and then move to Strongs, and get them to see all the possibilities.*

Examine the Strongs definition of the word:

> 7495 raphao { raw-faw'} or raphah { raw-faw'}
> a primitive root; 2196; v
> AV – heal 57, physician 5, cure 1, repaired 1, misc 3; 67
> Gk – 8324
> 1) to heal, make healthful
> 1a) (Qal) to heal
> 1a1) of God
> 1a2) healer, physician (of men)
> 1a3) of hurts of nations involving restored favour (fig)
> 1a4) of individual distresses (fig)
> 1b) (Niphal) to be healed
> 1b1) literal (of persons)
> 1b2) of water, pottery
> 1b3) of national hurts (fig)
> 1b4) of personal distress (fig)
> 1c) (Piel) to heal
> 1c1) literal
> 1c2) of national defects or hurts (fig)
> 1d) (Hithpael) in order to get healed (infinitive)

We are shown that it is God's very nature to heal as well as to bless. *Worship the LORD your God, and his blessing will be on your food and water. I will take away sickness from among you* (Exodus 23:25).

• What do we know of the promises of God?

The Old Testament is full of God's promises to bless, heal and sustain those who follow and keep his word, e.g. Psalm 41:3, *The Lord will sustain him on his sickbed and restore him from his bed of illness.* And Deuteronomy 7:12–15, *If you pay attention to these laws and are careful to follow them, then the Lord your God will keep his covenant of love with you, as he swore to your forefathers. He will love you and bless you and increase your numbers. He will bless the fruit of your womb, the crops of your land—your grain, new wine and oil—the calves of your herds and the lambs of your flocks in the land that he swore to your forefathers to give you. You will be blessed more than any other people; none of your men or women will be childless, nor any of your livestock without young. The Lord will keep you free from every disease. He will not inflict on you the horrible diseases you knew in Egypt, but he will inflict them on all who hate you.* —and so on.

There is always the proviso that we have to follow and keep his word, because the truth is in the word. The life is in the word. *My son, pay attention to what I say; listen closely to my words. Do not let them out of your sight, keep them within your heart; for they are life to those who find them and health to a man's whole body* (Proverbs 4:20–22).

Jesus told those who believed him that if they held to his teaching and really were his disciples they would know the truth and the truth would set them free. (See John 8:31f.) It is the word of truth, God's word, that sets us free, not our experience. The word tells us, *For nothing is impossible with God...* (Luke 1:37).

• *Ask the delegates to ask themselves these two questions and speak out the answers:*
1) Do I really believe that, or do I just toy with the idea?
2) Am I an indweller of the word, not only a reader and learner of the word?

The Jews are sometimes referred to as people of the book. Their history is also our history as Christians, but for us it is much more than that, much greater than that. Scripture is complete and cannot be added to, but we are told of another book: the Lamb's book of life, and we want to be 'overcomers' and find our names in that book. We are church, we are the body of Christ, corporately and individually. We who are born again are the temple of the living God. We know that some end-time events which have been prophesied in Scripture, and to which the Book of Revelation testifies, are still to happen. Almost two millennia have passed since the closure of the canonical Scripture, but your life and mine are vitally significant in terms of what God is doing in his kingdom, and we need to be aware that the words of Scripture are just as much alive and active in our everyday lives —now, as they were when they were first written. Do remember that we look forward to our names being in that book which belongs to God alone. (See Philippians 4:3 and Revelation 3:5). Heaven is watching each of us: so always remember that your life matters very much to God.

• **What did Jesus come to do?**
We recall again that Isaiah prophesied what Jesus was coming to do for us.

> *The Spirit of the Sovereign Lord is on me,*
> *because the Lord has anointed me*
> *to preach good news to the poor.*
> *He has sent me to bind up the brokenhearted,*

> *to proclaim freedom for the captives*
> *and release from darkness for the prisoners...*
> (Isaiah 61:1f)

—and how in Luke 4:1ff., following on from Jesus' baptism in water and the descent of the Holy Spirit upon him at that time, Jesus came out of the wilderness and returned to Galilee in the power of the Spirit. Then he entered the synagogue and applied that prophecy. *"The Spirit of the Lord is on me, because he has anointed me to preach good news to the poor. He has sent me to proclaim freedom for the prisoners and recovery of sight for the blind, to release the oppressed, to proclaim the year of the Lord's favour"* (Luke 4:18f.)

Jesus was stating clearly who he was and what he had come to do. He revealed, too, that he only did and said what he saw the Father do and say. It was clearly being proclaimed and demonstrated that it was his intention and will to preach the gospel of the kingdom, and to heal the sick. It is the will of Father God that the gospel is preached and the sick are healed.

• So, having said it, what did he do?

Having applied Isaiah's prophecy to himself, Jesus went on to prove he meant what he said. *Jesus left the synagogue and went to the home of Simon. Now Simon's mother-in-law was suffering from a high fever, and they asked Jesus to help her. So he bent over her and rebuked the fever, and it left her. She got up at once and began to wait on them. When the sun was setting, the people brought to Jesus all who had various kinds of sickness, and laying his hands on each one, he healed them* (Luke 4:38–40).

Jesus healed all who were brought to him. Matthew 8:17 teaches us that Jesus, in doing this, fulfilled the prophecy from Isaiah, that *he took up our infirmities and carried our diseases.*

Infirmities

769 astheneia { as-then'-i-ah}
from 772; TDNT - 1:490,83; n f
AV - infirmity 17, weakness 5, disease 1, sickness 1, 24
GK - 819
1) want of strength, weakness, infirmity
1a) of the body
1a1) its native weakness and frailty
1a2) feebleness of health or sickness
1b) of the soul
1b1) want of strength and capacity requisite
1b1a) to understand a thing
1b1b) to do things great and glorious
1b1c) to restrain corrupt desires
1b1d) to bear trials and troubles
3554 nosos { nos'–os}
of uncertain affinity; TDNT - 4:1091,655; n f
AV – disease 6, sickness 5, infirmity 1; 12
Gk – 3798
1) disease, sickness

The Greek words for 'infirmities' and 'diseases' mean just that – there is a full physical dimension to the meaning – but undoubtedly, when Jesus is present, spiritual and emotional implications are also encountered.

• What proof did he give John?

When John the Baptist was in prison, with his life in mortal danger, the question he had his disciples ask, 'Are you the one who was to come...?' suggests that he started to wonder whether he had misunderstood something. Was Jesus really the Messiah? That can maybe help those who are still seeking, and who may assailed by doubts. John was born to be the forerunner of Jesus. His father was told that he would be filled with the Holy Spirit even from birth (Luke 1:15), and when his expectant mother, Elizabeth, was visited by Mary, now pregnant with the baby Jesus, John 'leaped for joy' in his mother's womb. So he 'knew' Jesus even before they were both born. Then his life was devoted to telling people about the Messiah who was to come. His whole life was centred around preparing people to meet with Jesus. John baptised Jesus in water and stood there in the Jordan and was witness to God speaking from heaven, declaring that Jesus was his Son, in whom he was well pleased. John knew in his spirit, had seen with his eyes, and heard with his ears who Jesus was. Yet even he came to a time of questioning. So he sent his disciples to ask Jesus was he really the one who was to come! Jesus does not get upset. Jesus does not give a long theoretical answer. Remember, in his talks to the people, how Jesus used the imagery of being able to tell what kind of tree it is by the type of fruit it bears. He is teaching that you can tell what the nature of a man really is by what he does. So he replies to John in the same vein. The fruit demonstrates the truth: *Jesus replied, "Go back and report to John what you hear and see: The blind receive sight, the lame walk, those who have leprosy are cured, the deaf hear, the dead are raised, and the good news is preached to the poor"* (Matthew 11:4f).

• **What did he do for us?**

Often I get people saying that the salvation and healing on the cross is purely spiritual and emotional. They quote 1 Peter 2:24, *He himself bore our sins in his body on the tree, so that we might die to sins and live for righteousness; by his wounds you have been healed.* The Greek word used for stripe means a wound that trickles with blood. The word used for 'healed' here means to cure, to heal, to make whole in the physical sense, as well as referring to salvation. We are talking 'wholeness' in every sense. That is why so many of my friends involved in this ministry refer to it as a 'wholeness ministry'.

• Did Jesus demonstrate compassion and state his will?

When asked by the leper if he was willing to heal, Jesus stated that he was willing. Jesus is the same now as he was then and will be forever. So, if it was his will then, it is his will now.

When he came down from the mountainside, large crowds followed him. A man with leprosy came and knelt before him and said, "Lord, if you are willing, you can make me clean."

Jesus reached out his hand and touched the man. "I am willing," he said. "Be clean!" Immediately he was cured of his leprosy. Then Jesus said to him, "See that you don't tell anyone. But go, show yourself to the priest and offer the gift Moses commanded, as a testimony to them."

When Jesus had entered Capernaum, a centurion came to him, asking for help. "Lord," he said, "my servant lies at home paralyzed and in terrible suffering."

Jesus said to him, "I will go and heal him" (Matthew 8:1).

Filled with compassion, Jesus reached out his hand and touched the man. "I am willing," he said. "Be clean!" (Mark 1:41).

• How should we view doctors and medication?

I was talking with a Christian doctor friend (a general practitioner) about divine healing. He did not have a problem with the idea of Christian healing as such, but could not say that he believed that it was always God's will that people should be healed. So I posed a question that leads inexorably to a demonstration of the absurdity of that position, asking him how as a Christian he could continue to practise in a profession which led him continually into disobedience! The medical profession must operate on the assumption that healing or curing is good and is to be pursued. Does it make any kind of sense for Christians to hold that God sometimes wants people to remain unhealed? Scarcely, especially as we see throughout Scripture so much testimony to God's revealed will for healing. That doctor's way of thinking about God's will, had it been correct, would mean that in trying to help the patient he risks going against God's will in administering beneficial treatment! The same logic would apply to us all. If we do not think or feel that it is God's will that we get better, or if we think that God really gives us the illness or disability for some purpose (as some mistakenly suggest), then that would mean we should not seek to get better! On that erroneous premise we should not take any medication or do anything to alleviate the symptoms, as we would be going against God's will for us; we would be being disobedient, for, on that line of thinking, if it is not God's will that we should be healed then we should just get on and tolerate being sick and praise him for the sickness —not just praise him in our time of sickness but actually praise him for it. Needless to say, that would be a truly grotesque misunderstanding.

I hope very much you will agree with me that it is God's will to heal, so when we visit the doctor and take the medicine, and when we seek healing from God, we are acting in accordance with God's revealed will for us.

• Use the following two seemingly contradictory passages for open discussion

The apostles performed many miraculous signs and wonders among the people. And all the believers used to meet together in Solomon's Colonnade. No one else dared join them, even though they were highly regarded by the people. Nevertheless, more and more men and women believed in the Lord and *were added to their number. As a result, people brought the sick into the streets and laid them on beds and mats so that at least Peter's shadow might fall on some of them as he passed by. Crowds gathered also from the towns around Jerusalem, bringing their sick and those tormented by evil spirits, **and all of them were healed*** (Acts 5:12–16).

*And **he did not do many miracles there** because of their lack of faith* (Matthew 13:58).

Briefly—

The passage from Acts 8 follows directly on from the deaths of Ananias and Saphira when they lied to God and the Holy Spirit. As the disciples saw the result of their disobedience it says a great fear came upon the whole congregation – that is a fear of the Lord and fear of not keeping his word. As I see it, this fear of the Lord and desire to stay in his will, brought them so deeply into his righteousness that all who were brought to them were healed. The disciples were being transformed into the same image as Jesus as they moved from one degree of glory to the next. (2 Cor. 3:18)

This compares with:

*When evening came, many who were demon-possessed were brought to him, and he drove out the spirits with a word and **healed all the sick*** (Matthew 8:16).

I was once meditating on the Matthew 13 and wondering why Jesus did not do many miracles there and the Lord showed me how this situation could occur when Jesus was visiting his home town of Nazareth. There, the people who had known him and his family for years were making a great many disparaging remarks about him, his wisdom and his miraculous powers. Their incredulity and unbelief was so intense that most those who were sick simply did not come to him or were not brought to him. They did not come to the meeting. As we saw in Matthew 8:16 he healed all who were brought to him. Jesus does not change —he is the same today as he is tomorrow and so if he healed them all then he would heal them all the next time.

We know that the power to heal was present. I was once emailed by a friend who had been reading Luke 5:17, *One day as he was teaching, Pharisees and teachers of the law, who had come from every village of Galilee and from Judea and Jerusalem, were sitting there. And the power of the Lord was present for him to heal the sick.* This had led my friend to the understanding that the healing gift had to be 'Spirit driven' as he phrased it, and therefore could mean that there could be times with Jesus that the power would not be present for him to heal.

I replied: In some ways I would say that you are right that the power has to be present to heal. But the power comes with the anointing and as with Jesus the anointing comes with the Baptism in the Spirit. The receiving of the power from on high just as Jesus received at the side of the Jordan. Then he went through his time of testing as we all have to do from time to time. Next, according to Luke 4:14 he returned to Galilee in the power of the Spirit and started teaching the word. In verse 16 he came to Jerusalem and went into the synagogue where he read out verse18ff, *The Spirit of the Lord is upon me – He has anointed me*, etc, etc. If you read Isaiah 10:27 in AV (KJV), you see the secret —that it is the anointing that breaks the yoke. The anointing breaks the bondage to the oppressor.

On looking back again at Luke 5:17 you see that Jesus was teaching – he was preaching the word.

Check out Proverbs 4:20–23,

My son, pay attention to what I say;
listen closely to my words.
Do not let them out of your sight,
keep them within your heart;
for they are life to those who find them
and health to a man's whole body.
Above all else, guard your heart,
for it is the wellspring of life.

Healing – life – health – the issues of life itself are in the word. This is why Jesus commissioned us and instructed us to preach the word, preach that the kingdom is at hand. Life is in the word. Jesus is the word. Jesus is life.

When the Lord is present, the word is present —and the power is present. When we preach the word in the power of the Spirit then the power is present. The verse is showing that Jesus did not have to ask for the power to heal. Jesus did not have to seek for the power to heal. Where Jesus was, the power to heal was present. Even today, where Jesus **is**— the power to heal is present. Now look even further at who was there. Pharisees and teachers from every village in Galilee and Judea and from Jerusalem. This was some big meeting —some conspiracy, perhaps, for them to try and catch him out. These men were not there to sit at his feet as he was teaching and to receive the word. The Pharisees and the lawyers were there to judge and condemn. To my way of thinking, these men did not have little faith, not even no faith, these men in a way were negative faith. They were there to steal and destroy anything that Jesus did. We know from another passage, probably slightly earlier in Jesus' ministry, what happened when there was little faith present —there were few miracles.

In this verse the little faith is amongst his judges. I know myself how daunting it can be when amongst a group of clergy who are sceptical and ready to ridicule anything you do and say. It has happened to me many times. At those times I have to remember who has the power to heal —it is not me, it is Jesus. It is his authority in which we minister; therefore when we minister the word in faith then Jesus is present. And when Jesus is present, so is the power to heal. Does that make sense? Isn't it amazing how much one little verse is telling us?

So be encouraged by this verse, not discouraged. When and where you go in Jesus' name – under the anointing of the Holy Spirit – then, no matter who else is there, the power to heal is present. And as you look at the word power more closely, it is *dunamis* —it is MIGHTY POWER.

• Are healings miracles?

I see healing as 'spiritually natural'. The body is designed by God to heal itself. Healing is simply restoring the body, spirit and soul to God's original design. I see a miracle as being some event which, on a given occasion, works in a way completely different to the normal or to our expectation.

But so many live and work in hope not belief. Most of us know the story of what happened on the Emmaus Road: *"but we had hoped that he was the one who was going to redeem Israel. And what is more, it is the third day since all this took place"* (Luke 24:21).

When Jesus ministered, he did not move in hope that the people would be healed. He did not hope that Lazarus would come forth from the tomb —he knew that it was the Father's will. Until Pentecost and their coming into the anointing themselves the disciples moved in hope and not belief. Jesus speaks this out plainly to them:

He said to them, "How foolish you are, and how slow of heart to believe all that the prophets have spoken!" (Luke 24:25).

Many of us can get caught up with the excitement and the

hope, but that is not sufficient —that will let us down some time when all that we were hoping for – the healing we hoped for – is not manifested. We have to know that it is the will and nature of Jesus to heal. We have to know that, when Jesus said that he came to set the captives free and heal the sick, he meant every word of it. And when he said it was finished —then it was finished. He had accomplished all that he came to do. When the going gets tough, where will we be? In John 6, Jesus is telling them some hard facts about who he is. The disciples said (v 60), "This is a difficult statement; who can listen to it? *Aware that his disciples were grumbling about this, Jesus said to them, "Does this offend you?"* (John 6:61).

From this time many of his disciples turned back and no longer followed him (John 6:66).

We need to believe him.
We need to know it is his nature and will to heal.

MODULE 2

LISTENING TO OTHERS

Every good and perfect gift is from above, coming down from the Father of the heavenly lights, who does not change like shifting shadows. He chose to give us birth through the word of truth, that we might be a kind of first fruits of all he created. My dear brothers, take note of this: Everyone should be quick to listen, slow to speak and slow to become angry, for man's anger does not bring about the righteous life that God desires (James 1:17–20).

Throughout the session it needs to be stressed that it is most important to remember that, in listening, the other person is of paramount importance. We are not there to follow through any items on our own agenda.

Session 1
Ask the question: Why is it important to be a good listener? As they discuss the question, write their ideas up and make sure that the following points are brought out and highlighted, so people know they are being 'received' or attended to:
To allow the difficulties to surface;
To allow the healing needs to be revealed;
To facilitate resolution and healing;

To enable us to be conduits through whom the Holy Spirit flows into others.

Workshop 1
Exercise 1 in listening - Good for short term listening
Ask the class to do the following—
Choose a partner, someone you don't know.
Give a brief description of yourself —name and a few personal details. (3 minutes for each person.)
After each has a turn, repeat to your partner what you were told.
Check with your partner on how you did

Workshop 2
Exercise 2 in more intensive listening
Ask everyone in the class to write down 15 things about themselves in 5 minutes.

1	2
3	4
5	6
7	8
9	10
11	12
13	14
15	

Ask the class to choose a different partner from the last time.

Explain:
Partner 1 shares about themselves in conversational style (referring to list when necessary).
Partner 2 gives feedback on what he/she has heard.
As Partner 2 gives the feedback, partner 1 should tick off (in a way so that partner 2 giving the feedback cannot see) each of the 15 points that are covered. (15 minutes)
Change and repeat, so Partner 2 now shares and 1 listens, etc. (5 minutes)

Session 2
What are the skills needed for listening?
Preparation
Peaceful: Relaxed — Be 'prayed up; deal with distress or disturbance before you meet up with 'client'. Make sure you have no issues with unforgiveness, unbelief, unwillingness. (see Module 7, Be Clear for Prayer)

Responsiveness – Outward
Expressing availability – Welcoming: smile or gesture:
Look interested – nodding, affirming noises e.g. yes etc
Kindness
Contact:
Use of eye-to-eye contact.
Speech – 'I see': 'Oh, yes'; 'Mmmm.'
Physical touch – always make sure this is appropriate:
some people do not want any physical contact at all. Respect this.
Asking questions to clarify or to summarise ONLY.
Allowing silence.

Responsiveness – Inward

Listening to and watching for touch of the Holy Spirit, or when to give any words of knowledge etc.

Be alert to any personal issues rising up

Watchfulness

Body language —open/closed postures

Mixed signals e.g., smiling whilst recalling painful/shameful/frightening things.

Appearance —brightness; tearful; tense; heavy/depressed; unkempt; ill.

Listening or inattentive.

Flow of talk —fast; slow.

Communication of thoughts —muddled; clear; stilted; experiencing difficulty in sharing (could be fear, shame, embarrassment, etc.)

Session 3
What are the barriers to good listening?

(a) Judgementalism. Moral issues: lifestyles; personality conflicts. Things on which you have a particular view might come into conflict with your client. How do you listen without colluding or being judgmental?

(b) Self-awareness. Know when a personal unresolved agenda has been touched upon and how to put this on hold. Enables objectivity. (Be careful not to bury these, but to work through them at a later time.)

(c) Jumping to conclusions.

(d) Finishing off sentences; putting words into the other person's mouth. Not understanding, and guessing.

You should always check out, where you are not sure, where something is not clear.

You should always present your conclusion as a question

—checking out your understanding of what the person has said with their understanding of it.

(e) Lack of preparation

(f) Inattentiveness

(g) Overbusyness

(h) Tiredness

(i) Power/neediness issues (your own)

Allow 10 minutes for questions and comments

Suggested further reading:

Michael Jacobs *Swift to hear* (SPCK, 1985)

Joyce Huggett *Listening to Others*

Myra Chave-Jones *The Gift of Helping* (IV, 1982)

Roger Hurding *Roots and Shoots* (Hodder & Stoughton, 1985)

John and Paula Sandford *The Transformation of the Inner Man* (Logos, 1982)

MODULE 3

KNOWING OUR AUTHORITY IN JESUS

Although each of these modules is written to use as 'stand alone', they are all dependent on the acceptance that it is the nature and will of God to heal. Therefore, ask the delegates to give some indication as to why they accept this proposition.

Having established that it is God's nature and will to heal, and that it was Jesus' intention to accomplish this by his death on the cross, look at why we think that we should be able to continue in this work.

1. Therefore, accepting that it is God's nature and will to heal, we see from the following scriptures that it was his intention that Jesus would come into the world to make it possible for us to receive our healing through his death on the cross.

Here it was prophesied that on the cross Jesus would bear our griefs, our sorrows, our transgressions, our iniquities, and that by his wounds we would be healed: *Surely he took up our infirmities and carried our sorrows, yet we considered him stricken by God, smitten by him, and afflicted. But he was pierced for our transgressions, he was crushed for our iniquities; the punishment that brought us peace was upon him, and by his wounds we are healed. We all, like sheep, have gone astray, each of us has turned to his own way; and the LORD has laid on him the iniquity of us all* (Isaiah 53:4–6).

In 1 Peter 2:24 we get the confirmation that he bore our sins in his body, and that by his wounds we were healed. We then clearly see the difference between the work of the devil and the work that Jesus came to do.

In John 10:10 Jesus states, *"The thief comes only to steal and kill and destroy; I have come that they may have life, and have it to the full."* This is confirmed in 1 John 3:8. *"He who does what is sinful is of the devil, because the devil has been sinning from the beginning. The reason the Son of God appeared was to destroy the devil's work."*

And in Hebrews 2:14 we learn that Jesus shared in our humanity so that by his death he would destroy him who holds the power over death, that is the devil. It is recorded in John 19:28 that Jesus knew that all things had been accomplished in order that the Scripture might be fulfilled, and then he said, *"It is finished."* Then he bowed his head and gave up his spirit.

Following on from that, we need to be sure that we are able and have the authority to continue in this work. Ask the delegates to look up the references themselves and comment. Often there are differences of translation between Bibles, which are worth discussion.

2. Let us first look at the commission to the twelve, and the importance of the kingdom.

Jesus went through all the towns and villages, teaching in their synagogues, preaching the good news of the kingdom and healing every disease and sickness (Matthew 9:35).

He called his twelve disciples to him and gave them authority to drive out evil spirits and to heal every disease and sickness. These are the names of the twelve apostles: first, Simon (who is called Peter) and his brother Andrew; James son of Zebedee, and his brother John; Philip and Bartholomew; Thomas and Matthew the tax collector; James son of Alphaeus, and Thaddaeus; Simon the Zealot and Judas Iscariot, who betrayed him. These twelve Jesus sent out with the following instructions: "Do not go among the Gentiles or enter any town of the Samaritans. Go rather to the lost sheep of Israel. As you go, preach this message: 'The kingdom of heaven is near.' Heal the sick, raise the dead, cleanse those who have leprosy, drive out demons. Freely you have received, freely give. (Matthew 10:1–8)

When Jesus had called the Twelve together, he gave them power and authority to drive out all demons and to cure diseases, and he sent them out to preach the kingdom of God and to heal the sick. He told them: "Take nothing for the journey—no staff, no bag, no bread, no money, no extra tunic. Whatever house you enter, stay there until you leave that town. If people do not welcome you, shake the dust off your feet when you leave their town, as a testimony against them." So they set out and went from village to village, preaching the gospel and healing people everywhere (Luke 9:1–6).

3. Now what was the commission to the seventy-two?

After this the Lord appointed seventy-two others and sent them two by two ahead of him to every town and place where he was about to go. He told them, "The harvest is plentiful, but the workers are few. Ask the Lord of the harvest, therefore, to send out workers into his harvest field. Go! I am sending you out like lambs among wolves. Do not take a purse or bag or sandals; and do not greet anyone on the road. When you enter a house, first say, 'Peace to this house.' If a man of peace is there, your peace will rest on him; if not, it will return to you. Stay in that house, eating and drinking whatever they give you, for the worker deserves his wages. Do not move around from house to house. When you enter a town and are welcomed, eat what is set before you. Heal the sick who are there and tell them, 'The kingdom of God is near you.' (Luke 10:1–9).

In both the Luke commissions – to the twelve and the seventy-two – it is interesting to note his emphasis that they should go out being totally reliant on him, taking nothing of their own —bag, purse, money, etc. You may find that some versions of the Bible put the number at 70 and some at 72.

4. What was the commission to the disciples?

When they saw him, they worshiped him; but some doubted. Then Jesus came to them and said, "All authority in heaven and on earth has been given to me. Therefore go and make disciples of all nations, baptizing them in the name of the Father and of the Son and of the Holy Spirit, and teaching them to obey everything I have commanded you. And surely I am with you always, to the very end of the age" (Matthew 28:17–20).

The instruction is to make disciples of men not to go and save men. Oswald Chambers makes the point that being a disciple is not a self development programme but a self denial programme so that with less of us we can become more of him and therefore more able to move in his authority. *For whoever wants to save his life will lose it, but whoever loses his life for me will find it* (Matthew 16:25).

5. And what were the disciples to do?

He said to them, "Go into all the world and preach the good news to all creation. Whoever believes and is baptized will be saved, but whoever does not believe will be condemned. And these signs will accompany those who believe: In my name they will drive out demons; they will speak in new tongues; they will pick up snakes with their hands; and when they drink deadly poison, it will not hurt them at all; they will place their hands on sick people, and they will get well."

After the Lord Jesus had spoken to them, he was taken up into heaven and he sat at the right hand of God. Then the disciples went out and preached everywhere, and the Lord worked with them and confirmed his word by the signs that accompanied it (Mark 16:15–20).

Basically they were to go and preach the gospel and heal the sick and expect the signs and miracles to follow them.

6. *Discuss what the Bible means by a believer*

In Mark 16:15ff we see that he taught that believers would lay hands on the sick, who would recover. We need to know that we follow in that line of authority and commissioning. So, if we are to continue in his ministry of healing, we have to know that we truly are believers. It is not only a matter of believing in God and who Jesus is. We are told in James 2:19 that even the demons believe there is one God —and shudder. To me, it goes deeper than believing in Jesus as Lord, to a point that we need to be able to say, 'yes', if we are asked the question, 'Do you believe Jesus?' —Not just believe who Jesus is; not just believe in Jesus but actually believe him and his word to the point that you are willing to step out and do what he tells us to. *"And you do not have his word abiding in you, for you do not believe him whom he sent"* (John 5:38). *"I tell you the truth, whoever hears my word and believes him who sent me has eternal life and will not be condemned; he has crossed over from death to life"* (John 5:24). Here Jesus draws together the concept of believing his word and believing in God the Father. Do you believe that we can cast out demons, speak with new tongues, and lay hands on the sick (and they will recover)? Jesus goes even further than this in John 14:12, *I tell you the truth, anyone who has faith in me will do what I have been doing. He will do even greater things than these, because I am going to the Father.*

Encourage everyone for homework to do a word study in the New Testament on 'believes'.

7. What does Jesus say about being born again?

It would appear that to be in his ministry of healing I initially need to know two things about myself: that I am a believer, and that I am born again. Jesus declared, *"I tell you the truth, no one can see the kingdom of God unless he is born again"* (John 3:3). I need to know and claim for myself the promises that are involved in being a born again believer, such as these:

1. That I have eternal life. (See John 5:24.)
2. That nothing can separate me from the love of God in Christ Jesus. (See Romans 8:38f.)
3. That he will do whatever I ask in Jesus' name. (See John 14:13.)
4. With faith even as small as a mustard seed, nothing will be impossible for me. (See Matthew 17:20.)
5. That I am a member of a holy priesthood. (See 1 Peter 2:5.)
6. That I am called as a saint. (Romans 1:7.)

I could go on and on reciting promise after promise of who the Scriptures say that I am in Christ Jesus, the promises that come with being a born again believer. I need to have the authority of who I am in Jesus written all through me, so that when it is necessary I can stand without fear or doubt against the wiles and deceit and force of the enemy. Then I know that Satan has to flee. (See James 4:7.)

One day, during a time of uncertainty in my life, God showed me a picture of a stick of candy rock. Usually these sticks of candy have the name of a holiday town written all the way through them in colour. Father told me to look at this stick of candy. I saw written through it, 'Randolph, son of God'. That is who and what you are, he told me. And no matter what happens to that stick of candy, whether it is snapped in half, sucked to the bottom, or broken into pieces, it will still say 'Randolph, son of God', right through the middle of it.

In this ministry we need that confidence as to our sonship and authority in Jesus, and this must be evident in the way we minister, for: *In this way, love is made complete among us so that we will have confidence on the day of judgement, because in this world we are like him* (1 John 4:17). So the love we show is to be like the love Jesus showed.

We need to know that we are Christians. Many years ago, a senior colleague was arguing with me about the fact that I had dismissed one of our managers. I had apologised for not informing him beforehand. He looked at me and said, "And you call yourself a Christian."

I was just about to let that go when I stopped and replied, "I don't call myself a Christian, I am a Christian. I might not always act like a good one but nothing can take away the fact that I am one."

8. What work does God ask a believer to do?
Ask the delegates this question, and see if anyone gets close to the answer.

Having established that I am a believer, I have to know what the central work of a believer is. What do I have to do? Jesus said, *"The work of God is this: to believe in the one he has sent"* (John 6:29). That is so simple. Nothing complicated. Our job is to believe in Jesus, and everything else will flow out from that.

9. When did Jesus start to heal?

In the reference to the time when Jesus, as a youth, stayed on in Jerusalem, listening to and questioning the teachers whilst his parents were journeying home, we are clearly given the impression that Jesus appeared wise beyond his years. In the passage he also obliquely referred to God as his father but there is no evidence that Jesus performed any miracles or did any healings until after he was thirty years of age and was baptised in water and the Spirit.

In Module 1, we noted that, after the descent of the Holy Spirit upon him at the Jordan and his time in the wilderness, he went into the temple and claimed the prophecy from Isaiah 61:1 for himself. *"The Spirit of the Lord is on me, because he has anointed me to preach good news to the poor. He has sent me to proclaim freedom for the prisoners and recovery of sight for the blind, to release the oppressed, to proclaim the year of the Lord's favour"* (Luke 4:18f).

We can now see that it was not until after this that any miracles or healings by Jesus are recorded. Something very special, very powerful, occurred on the banks of the Jordan —where we are told that the Holy Spirit descended on him in bodily form like a dove. (See Luke 3:22f.) *And a voice came from heaven: "You are my Son, whom I love; with you I am well pleased."* In Luke 4:14, we are told that Jesus returned to Galilee in the power of the Spirit and news about him spread through the whole countryside. Then in the temple he makes the declaration in his quotation from Isaiah, which includes the affirmation that he (Jesus) was now anointed to preach and heal. *"The Spirit of the Lord is on me, because he has anointed me to preach good news to the poor. He has sent me to proclaim freedom for the prisoners and recovery of sight for the blind, to release the oppressed"* (Luke 4:18).

This is the first time in the Bible that the concepts of the power and anointing of the Holy Spirit come together. When he agreed to come to earth as man we know that he came, just like us, without heavenly powers —because he made himself nothing, taking the very nature of a servant, being made in human likeness. (See Philippians 2:7). He laid aside – he stripped himself – of his mighty power and glory but that does not mean that he also laid aside his divine nature. Jesus was 100% man and also 100% divine. If he had come in his pre-incarnate state with all his power, he would not have needed this new anointing. God is the anointing one – he does not need to be anointed – but in this aspect Jesus was also 100% man like us and needed to be anointed in power.

10. What did Jesus promise us?
He told the disciples to stay in Jerusalem until they received the same Holy Spirit. "I am going to send you what my Father has promised; but stay in the city until you have been clothed with power from on high" (Luke 24:49).

The activity of the Holy Spirit is referred to in the Scriptures in a number of ways. *Ask the delegates if they can name some of these ways.*
1. Promise of the Father. (Luke 24:49; Acts 1:4; Acts 2:33.)
2. Gift of the Spirit. (Acts 2:38.)
3. Baptised in the Spirit. (John 1:33; Acts 1:5; Acts 11:16.)
4. Receiving the Holy Spirit. (Acts 8:17; Acts 10:47; Acts 19:2.)
5. Filled with the Spirit. (Acts 2:4; Acts 9:17.)
6. Coming upon. (Luke 1:35.)
7. Clothed with power. (Luke 24:49.)
8. Falling upon. (Acts 10:44; Acts 11:15.)
9. Poured out. (Acts 2:33; Acts 10:45.)

11. What does the anointing do?

In that day their burden will be lifted from your shoulders, their yoke from your neck; the yoke will be broken because you have grown so fat (Isaiah 10:27).

Isaiah 10:27 (in the Authorised Version) tells us that the yoke will be destroyed because of the anointing. The word *shemen* is used 190 times in the bible and signifies grease, liquid, olive oil, the anointing oil. In the translations which use 'fatness' this is speaking metaphorically of a fat bull, which has grown so strong it breaks away from its yoke. No longer does it have to go round and round, yoked to the treadmill; it breaks free. Now that is power —power to break the yoke. The anointing power from on high.

Today we can have all kinds of yokes that need to be broken so that we and the people to whom we minister can be set free —sickness, depression, poverty, spiritual blindness, bitterness, rejection, lonliness, grief, and so on. Jesus in his ministry after the anointing went on to release all those who came to him from these yokes of oppression. Stress to the delegates that it is imperative that they know that they are baptised in the Holy Spirit —that they are anointed.

We have seen that the anointing breaks the yoke of oppression. We know that Jesus came to heal the sick, and that he did so. We know that Jesus has authority over everything. He said, *"All authority in heaven and on earth has been given to me"* (Matthew 28:18). The authority he gave to his followers in the commissions is the same authority he has given to us. He entrusted power to them to minister healing, and he entrusts it to us too.

In fact, the Scriptures go even further: *In this way, love is made complete among us so that we will have confidence on the day of judgment, because in this world we are like him* (1 John 4:17).

12. Theologies of healing and the centrality of the kingdom now.

Ask the delegates if they can think of any theologies of healing of which they have heard.

Here are a few on which I shall comment:

> Dispensational theology (Luther, etc.)
> Experiential theology
> Intervention theology
> Name others:
> Pragmatic (George Bennet)
> Holistic
> Trinitarian
> Sacramental, etc.

A funnel of love. That is what the Lord showed me that I was to be. That is the picture that he gave to me of the Christian's role in Jesus' ministry of healing —a funnel through which he can pour his love, and peace, and grace and healing power into those who need him.

I suppose that I possibly got the first glimpse of this when my wife Dorothy and I were in a position where we could not speak the language of the people to whom we were ministering. We happened to be in Germany, in East Berlin, and we did not speak any German. This was way before the Berlin Wall was destroyed and we had entered the eastern part of the city through 'Checkpoint Charlie'. Our host, guide and interpreter was my friend Jean Pierre Witzman, the Berlin President of the Full Gospel Businessmens' Fellowship International (FGB).

In those days in East Berlin, any meeting that had anything at all to do with things religious had, by law, to be held in a building specifically licensed for religious gatherings. Normally FGB meetings were held in restaurants or hotels, in association with a good meal. This meeting was in a small church, without heating, and with just a cup of coffee. I remember it was cold in that church, and everyone kept their coats on. After worship and my talk, we came to a time for ministry. Jean Pierre announced in German that anyone who required prayer should come forward. It was a small room and it was packed with people. Some space was made in the front. A little elderly lady shuffled forward. All her joints were stiff and she could not walk, only shuffle. She spoke no English, and Jean Pierre was occupied with other people. Therefore I simply laid hands on her by gently holding her shoulders. The Lord showed me how cold and desolate she was inside, not physically cold because of the temperature of the room, but emotionally and spiritually frozen. It felt like a cold, devastated wasteland inside of her, with no hope. I was filled with the understanding that all she had loved and cared for had been taken away from her.

I asked Dorothy to hold her. Dorothy is only five feet two inches tall, but she was considerably taller than this round little woman, and was able to wrap her arms around the lady and cuddle her. Neither Dorothy nor I spoke aloud —there was no point, she would not have understood us. We prayed silently in tongues. Dorothy held her for what seemed a very long time until she felt that the Lord had done all that was necessary. As Dorothy held the lady, Father God poured love and warmth and hope and peace, and who knows what more, into her very being —and quickened and released her imprisoned spirit. At this time we had not yet learned all that we would come to understand about the need, and the ways in which we are able to minister to the human spirit, but through his grace this was not a problem. All that was required of us was to be there and be willing to be his arms, so that he could love her back to life. By twisting and wriggling our bodies, we demonstrated that we wanted her to wriggle and move. As she wriggled, she realised that the love of God had brought warmth and healing into the frozen wasteland within her, that her very joints and bones had been unfrozen and she had been set free. When she went back to her place in the congregation, she did not shuffle but walked freely. One of the lasting impressions in my mind, and I do not think I will ever forget it, took place after the meeting had finished and everyone was leaving. The little lady, whose name we never even knew, turned her head when she got to the door, looked over her shoulder, smiled at us with a merry twinkle in her eye and then cheekily wiggled her bottom at us to show she was healed and free. It was like the description in Malachi 4:2, *But for you who revere my name, the sun of righteousness will rise with healing in its wings. And you will go out and leap like calves released from the stall.* This little, round, elderly lady literally skipped out of the room.

In retrospect, I realised that this was the first glimmerings of what many years later I was to call 'Absorption Theology'. I realised that the great gift that we can bring to people is the overwhelming presence of God's love, in the power of the Holy Spirit. Their healing comes through soaking in the anointing of the Holy Spirit, so that they simply absorb into their very being the healing love of Jesus, without their needing to be aware or their brain have any understanding of what is happening. Healing is absorbing into our spirit, soul and body all the wonderful gifts that Jesus won for us on the cross and has stored up for us in heaven. I cannot heal anyone. Although God has given our bodies the natural ability to heal, we cannot consciously heal ourselves. It is the very nature and will of God to heal. He does the healing; we soak it in and absorb it.

He finally showed me the picture of us as a funnel of love. Well, in fact, not the complete funnel but as our arms go round someone in need, they form the narrow opening at the end of the funnel. Can you picture the kind of funnel he showed me? The sort of funnel used to pour oil from a can into the car engine, or to pour any liquid from a large container into a bottle.

Part of the vision that the Lord gave me for setting up the Northumbrian Centre of Prayer for Christian Healing, here in Beggars Roost, was to teach and encourage the body of Christ at large to embrace his ministry of healing. This would entail going out to other churches and congregations both here and overseas, as we were invited.

Over the years I had observed the reasons why few churches and congregations became involved with healing. Their main concern, which they voiced, was, 'But what about the ones who don't get healed?' It appeared to them that to accept a theology for healing meant accepting a God who was partial, and who chose to intervene beneficially in the lives of some but not of others. whereas the Scriptures tell us that God is impartial. Even the Pharisees knew that about Jesus. *Then the Pharisees went and counselled together how they might trap him in what he said. And they sent their disciples to him, along with the Herodians, saying, "Teacher, we know that you are truthful and teach the way of God in truth, and defer to no one; for you are not partial to any* (Matthew 22:15f, NASB).

Then Peter began to speak: "I now realize how true it is that God does not show favouritism... (Acts 10:34). And Paul also writes, *For God does not show favouritism* (Romans 2:11).

The truth of the Scriptures contradicted the experience of the churches. Therefore it was safer not to get involved with healing in the first place. Isn't it strange that people do not have the same problem in relation to doctors? The evidence is that many people who undergo medical treatment do not get well, and many die, but no one suggests that we should therefore stop going to consult the physician. I once read that during a doctors' strike in Israel the death rate fell by 50%. I also began to understand why few churches embrace Jesus' statement in

Mark 16:16–18 that those who have believed will lay hands on the sick and they will recover. I realised that the main reason is fear. There is very poor teaching and understanding in the churches regarding the relationship between faith and healing. The ministers are fearful that if they lay hands on the sick and they are not seen to recover, then what is this saying about the faith and belief of the minister in front of the whole congregation? Then there is fear from those who are sick. Fear that if they go forward for prayer and do not get healed, then what is this saying about their own faith? How will it look in the eyes of others? Especially if they know of someone else who was healed. They feel that the comparison would be odious. Therefore it is safer to sit in the pew and cope with the problem. It is safer to stay sick and not take the chance. If that were truly the case about healing and faith and God it would be odious. (I will deal with the place of faith in healing later on.)

All of this made me eager to know as much as I could about Jesus' ministry of healing and to compare different understandings. Could we really expect to see healing today? There are many 'theologies' centred around healing and or the gifts of the Spirit and I will very briefly refer to a few. There are, for instance, the 'dispensational' theologians, from Luther onwards, who think that God only allowed healing, together with the gifts of the Spirit, for the times of the early church.

Then there are many ministers who follow an 'experiential' line of theology. Their belief is retrospective. Perhaps they can recall a situation when they prayed for someone who had a headache, for example, and the headache went. Now it is their experience that prayer can heal headaches —so they have no problem praying with a parishioner who has headaches. However, as they have never experienced someone with Parkinson's disease being healed, they would never dream of laying hands on such a person.

It always amuses me that whole church congregations can have a set time of intercessions where they can pray for amazingly big things to happen —such as praying for floods in Bangladesh to subside and all the people be saved. They can pray for the wellbeing of people in hospital. But actually to lay hands on someone in front of the congregation and expect them to be healed —this is too much in the now; too much of an 'in your face' ministry, because, if they do not immediately get better, you are actually still there with the sick in front of you, still sick.

It is much the same with some of my friends who can believe that Jesus came to save the world —and they can pray for and expect for salvation. They can believe for eternal life, but not for healing the sick, which Jesus also came to do. Is it because eternal life is an easier concept to accommodate, because you do not have to test it out until after you are dead? If the person does not immediately confess their sins and ask Jesus into their lives, my friends do not give up on them and say that salvation does not work, that salvation is not for now, or that Jesus did not come that all might be saved. No, they know that Jesus came for the whole world, so they are spurred on to greater efforts to pray even more fervently for the one who is lost. This is much less stressful than healing now. Is this why many of our evangelical friends preach from the dispensational agenda?

Then we have what I class as the 'pragmatic' theologians of whom I consider The Revd. George Bennett to be my favourite. In his book *Miracle at Crowhurst* he describes how he laid hands on the sick and expected them to recover for no other reason than because Jesus said we should. No frills, no fancy wrappings and theological explanations other than the simple fact that this what Jesus says we should do. Basically I am with George Bennett. As you will see, although God has shown me this 'funnel of love' and a multitude and variety of ways to pray and minister to people, they are all just part and parcel of Jesus' exhortation to those who believe (as in Mark 16). I consider myself to one of those who has believed, and later you will get a somewhat clearer idea of what I mean by 'believe'.

There are those with a 'sacramental' theological view on healing. They consider that the healing is effected in the receiving of the body and blood of Christ during the celebration of communion. I have no quarrel with this, but it is not one of the models that Jesus or the disciples used in the Scriptures. There we see Jesus using many very different ways of ministering to the needs of people.

As I thought about interventionist ideas, I had a picture in my mind, as I have inadequately shown in the figure, of God sitting up in heaven, way above the problems of man. Then, as he looked down and saw some situation he desired to change, down shot this lightning bolt of assistance into the affairs of man, to the benefit of those he wanted to help. I realised that this is the way so many see God, and why they pray the way that they do. But this was not my conception of Father. As I read and studied more, I was impressed with the importance of the 'kingdom' and its relationship with healing. For example: *Jesus went throughout Galilee, teaching in their synagogues, preaching the good news of the kingdom, and healing every disease and sickness among the people* (Matthew 4:23).

The gospel of the kingdom is central to Jesus' teaching and ministry. I realised that he was not just talking about a kingdom that was to come some time in the future, simply some eschatological experience in which we will also be made whole and released from all sickness and disease. No, this was and is a 'now' thing. *"The time has come,"* he said. *"The kingdom of God is near. Repent and believe the good news!"* (Mark 1:15.)

The kingdom of God is at hand —this did not mean it was coming soon, nor that Jesus was saying that this is just a 'trailer' for the feature film to be released after the Second Coming. No, he was talking about the there and then – the here and now. What would I do if say I decided to bake a cake? I would check that I had all the ingredients and lay them out on the kitchen counter. I would get out the tools I would need – the spoons, the whisk, the cake tins, etc – and when they were all collected together in a convenient place I would start to mix the cake. I would not start until everything was at hand where I could just reach out and pick what I need as I require it. No running around frantically, wondering do I have this or that ingredient, and trying to remember where I had possibly put the egg whisk last time I used it, or even— do I have one? Everything would be at hand. The same would apply if I were going to do a job around the house. Some time ago someone gave me one of those wonderful tool belts. Before doing any job I get the tool belt, make sure the hammer, the pliers, the screwdrivers and so on are all in place before I move to the job. Then I know that all that I will need to complete that job is at hand. All I have to do is reach out and take hold of it. I do not have to wonder whether I have a this, or a that, which is imperative for a fruitful completion and successful outcome. I know that I have all that I need, and it is all at hand. This is the gospel of the kingdom that Jesus was proclaiming. We have all that we need and it is readily at hand, and all we have to do is reach out and get hold of it and use it, because those who born again should realise that they have the privilege of living in the kingdom now. I heard one well-known evangelist who advocated healing, describing it as borrowing it from the kingdom that is to come when Jesus comes back to rule on the earth. He has missed the promise that we do not have to borrow from the future when we live in the kingdom now. Dorothy and I teach seminars on living in the kingdom.

Just look at what some others say about the kingdom. Jean Darnell describes it as life in the overlap. Schweitzer called it the 'interim ethic'. Gustaf Aulen said, 'Justification is simply the atonement brought into the present so that here and now the blessing of God prevails over the curse.' J. V. Taylor postulated, 'If a theology of hope means that we lose our assurance of the already givenness of the kingdom then it is defective.' Alan Ecclestone stated that, 'The kingdom signified a life to be laid hold of now, within the kingdoms of the earth.' J. A. T. Robinson wrote, 'The koinonia or common ownership of the Holy Spirit was the distinctive thrilling announcement of the new age with the Holy Spirit as the window into everything that God in Christ means for us.'

On the other hand there are theologians such as Kummel who disagree with this concept. He considered it all eschatological. J.A.T. Robinson's fascinating image of the Holy Spirit as the window into heaven tied in completely with my understanding of 'us' as being the narrow opening at the end of the funnel of love. I have tried to draw this in the figure below, as the alternative to – or the correction of – the interventionist theology. God indeed is in his heaven, way above the problems of man, but stored up alongside is all that Jesus won for us on the cross. All the healing and deliverance from sickness and sin, all the abundance of life that he promised —he came that we might have it. And it is there ready to be poured out upon us, and into us, as we can receive it. As Robinson suggests, the window (or in my case the funnel) into heaven through which Jesus can pour this is made possible by the Holy Spirit. When one of us, filled and anointed in the Holy Spirit, stands there beside those in need with our arms around them, we become part of the funnel that can direct the flow of love on to and into those who need it.

The first half of the diagram depicts Intervention Theology with God showing partiality in intervening in human needs.

In the diagram on Absorption theology 'the age past' comes before the cross, then comes 'the present age' for those in Christ (the kingdom now); then 'the age to come', when Christ comes again. Even though they are alive with us now, I would consider that those people who do not know Jesus as Lord are governed under the laws of the 'age past'. They can benefit greatly from the signs and wonders that follow those who believe.

Make a transparency of this diagram so that it can be projected on a screen.

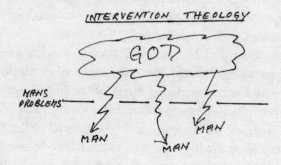

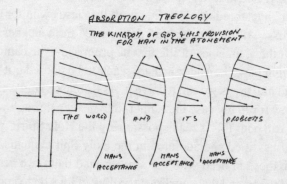

13. Do you know about the word and believe it?

The truth is in the word — *rhema*.

The life is in the word *...for they are life to those who find them and health to the whole body.*

Read Proverbs 4:20-27. It is the word that sets us free.

What does the word say? NOT experience.

Nothing is impossible to God. Do I believe that?

It is Jesus' will that we are healed. Jesus came to destroy the works of the devil, and when we minister in Jesus' name, in his love, we are doing as he did. We have noted already that according to John 14:12 the disciples were to do even greater things (than the miracles or works he did in his earthly ministry, depending on which translation is used). So in Jesus' name, operating in his love, the authority, power and will to heal is ours, and when we encounter the results of the activity of the devil, we enter that spiritual warfare covered by the victory Jesus won on the cross. He defeated Satan.

MODULE 4

GIFTS OF THE SPIRIT

The Anointing to Heal contains many illustrations of the use and definition of the gifts of the Spirit, which can be used when teaching this module. Chapter six of the book particularly focuses on the use of the prophetic gifts.

Gifts of the Spirit

Ask the delegates to take about ten minutes to write down as many answers as possible to the following:
(1) To give their definition of 'gifts of the Spirit'
(2) When was the Spirit first given to the church?
(3) How many gifts of the Spirit can they name?

Bring them back together and, in order, share and discuss the answers to number (3), and write them up for all to see.

Gifts
Ask them to search these scriptures listed below, and name the gifts they find. As they call them out, check them against the list already written up and add the new ones, if any. Obviously you need to give them a list of the Scripture verses which does not show the answers.

Acts 2:1–4	(other tongues)
Romans 5:16–18	(righteousness)
Romans 6:23	(eternal life)
Romans 12:6–8	(prophecy, service, teaching, exhortation, giving, leading, mercy)
1 Cor 12:1–31	(wisdom, word of knowledge, faith, healing, miracles, prophecy, discernment of spirits, tongues, interpretation of tongues —then apostles, prophets, teachers, miracle workers, gifts of helps, administrations – healings, tongues, interpretation)
Eph 4:11–13	(apostles, prophets, evangelists, pastors, teachers)
Heb 2:4	(miracles and gifts of the Holy Spirit)
Heb 13:20–21	(every good thing)
1Cor 14:22	(tongues, prophecy)
Eph 3:10	(manifold wisdom of God)
2Tim 1:6	(the gift of God which is in you)

Ask them to say:
—which gift(s) they have received
—been given
—How and when do they use it (them)?
—Do they desire other gifts?

Gifts (spiritual)

We shall look at the gifts of the Spirit in the context of being equipped by God to minister to others where we are – in our local church – in other words, the Body of Christ in action. In

Ezekiel 11:19f we read of this provision: *I will give them an undivided heart and put a new spirit in them; I will remove from them their heart of stone and give them a heart of flesh. Then they will follow my decrees and be careful to keep my laws. They will be my people, and I will be their God.*

The wonderful thing about this to me is the sense of belonging: *They will be my people.* Joel 2:28f reiterates this, *'And afterward, I will pour out my Spirit on all people. Your sons and daughters will prophesy, your old men will dream dreams, your young men will see visions. Even on my servants, both men and women, I will pour out my Spirit in those days.* Again this sense of belonging — my Spirit on my people. Both prophets were prophesying about the Spirit of God impacting mankind, with the possibility of new birth and the spiritual equipping to live in the power of the Holy Spirit being given, and we know this started at Pentecost, when he did indeed come in a demonstration of presence and power, and birthed the Church as described in Acts 2:1-4. *When the day of Pentecost came, they were all together in one place. Suddenly a sound like the blowing of a violent wind came from heaven and filled the whole house where they were sitting. They saw what seemed to be tongues of fire that separated and came to rest on each of them. All of them were filled with the Holy Spirit and began to speak in other tongues as the Spirit enabled them.*

Our purpose

The purpose of the Church is to be the temple of God here on earth. *What agreement is there between the temple of God and idols? For we are the temple of the living God. As God has said: "I will live with them and walk among them, and I will be their God, and they will be my people"* (2Cor 6:16).

The function of its members is—

First to believe in Jesus whom God sent, and through whom they have his life. *Jesus answered, "The work of God is this: to believe in the one he has sent"* (John 6:29). We believe Jesus first and then we turn to others to serve everybody else in our orbit. Believe God first; give him prime place, and then turn to be a servant of everybody —whoever touches our life or whoever's life we touch. And the way we serve is by telling out the good news.

Secondly we are to share this good news by telling it to others and by witnessing to it through our lifestyles. *He said to them, "Go into all the world and preach the good news to all creation"* (Mark 16;15ff). Remember that wherever we are, whatever we do, we are witnessing to something. We are either witnessing to the 'Christ life' within us or we are witnessing to the lack of 'Christ life' within us —there are no other choices. We have two positions: we are either in Jesus are we are not in Jesus. For instance, if somebody does something cruel to us that hurts us and we think 'Right, I will get them back for that', then we are not in Jesus. That is not a response of the Lord, and in those instances the Holy Spirit is showing where we have need of him. He will use every circumstance. 'All things work together for good....' I used to think that meant that everything was going to become easier and more pleasant because I loved God and I was called according to his plans. What I came to realise was that even amidst the most rotten, grotty things that were happening there was something that he was using for good. Part of that is to show us where we trust him, believe him, respond like him —and where we do not. Both findings are good; both are a treasure.

We need to be thankful in whatever situation we are in, and realise that in the past we may not have responded as we should have done. In adverse circumstances, if we have not responded like Jesus, then we can say, 'Thank you for showing me my need.' We do not go off into condemnation, but we stay with the Lord and his view, his way of doing things. So we are always witnessing to something.

Thirdly, we are to love and serve one another wherever and however that is necessary, through the power of the Holy Spirit and in the ways he leads us to do so. *"This is my command: Love each other"* (John 15:17). In other words, the needs and demands we meet with in our everyday lives, and in interacting with others, will usually demonstrate where this Spirit life is, or where it is needed by us, or needed to be released through us towards others. This is the most usual way of finding out what is usually called 'my ministry'. We do not have to know what our ministry is, we will find out as we go. We do not even have to label it. It is an error to think that we do not have a ministry. The ministry we have is the ministry of reconciliation. *We are therefore Christ's ambassadors, as though God were making his appeal through us. We implore you on Christ's behalf: Be reconciled to God* (2 Corinthians 5:20).

He has given us this ministry of reconciliation. So that means starting with me —where am I not reconciled to God? Where am not able to live in reconciliation with any other person on the planet? We start from there. We so often want to go and have a ministry to do for the Lord which will take us away from all of that, because it is uncomfortable and unpleasant to actually face the reality of the way that we are without him. John is quite clear: if we say we have no sin we deceive ourselves the truth is not in us. So you can see it is just a matter of spiritual commonsense to know that the Holy Spirit is going to be showing us when we are open to him. You can sit with him when you go home, and say, 'Can we just have a little review of the day Lord? Will you show me where I walked with you, and where I didn't? So often we are afraid to do that because we are afraid to find out where he says, 'Well, you didn't', or we do not want to change. You know that he is going to touch on that topic where you had a bit of a ding-dong with so and so. And I am not ready to put it right yet —so it is no use my talking to the Holy Spirit. I do not want to talk to him about it. He will just bring up the same old thing: Give in – forgive – let go, and so on. Sometimes we are afraid to go to God because we fear what he might show us. This is always a place of lack of trust and not being in Jesus. We need the Spirit every second of every single minute. There is not a time when we can have a day off from the Lord!

This, then, is how the Body of Christ, the church on earth, is meant to function, each one working under his authority; and knowing one's position as a part of his body in his plan of redemption, restoration and healing to wholeness. This is a Holy Spirit centred life —one we all have to be nurtured in, taught about and grow in. God does this by interacting with us, and through his active, indwelling presence with us. There are what are termed in Scripture 'gifts of the Spirit' —in other words, gifts from himself. He is not a tongue, but the tongue is of him. He is not a healing, but the healing is of him. Once we are born again, initially it is not easy to grasp fully that we are in the Spirit. So, teaching us about his being our protector, God inspired Paul to write that wonderful passage in Ephesians about putting on the full armour of God. He described the armour that a Roman soldier would wear, because we can look at it piece by piece and get hold of it, and have a picture of it, so that our understanding grows. Then, when he makes it revelation to us, at that point the pieces are put down and we stay with the wholeness of the Lord. Not notions of the Lord — not thoughts about God, but being with God.

From the many gifts we unearthed earlier, we want to concentrate on what (in 1 Corinthians 12) Paul refers to as the spiritual gifts. When we are baptised in the Holy Spirit we are filled with the Holy Spirit. The gifts belong to the Holy Spirit. We never own these gifts; they are never *our* gifts. He simply enables us to move in his gifts. Therefore, when we are filled with the Holy Spirit we can use all the gifts. We are all filled with the same Holy Spirit. For example, no-one receives a mute Holy Spirit, therefore we can all speak in tongues. The fact that we might not have used the gift of tongues does not mean that we cannot speak in tongues, but simply that we are not using the gift. Whereas in fact he wants us all to speak in tongues, because tongues is the only gift which is for us, for our edification, for building us up.

We now consider the nine gifts listed in 1Corinthians 12, in three groups: gifts of utterance; gifts of power; gifts of revelation. Each group contains three gifts.

1. Gifts of Utterance

Tongues

For anyone who speaks in a tongue does not speak to men but to God. Indeed, no one understands him; he utters mysteries with his Spirit (1Corinthians 14:2).

This gift is given to an individual so that God may build us up in the life of his Spirit. When we use it, we are in effect using what is of God, and as we do so he grows us or edifies us. Paul called it the least of the gifts. He did not mean that it is worth nothing or hardly anything compared to the other gifts. What he meant was that it should seem the most usual thing to us. The least in the sense that we should just move in the Lord like this. Talk in the Lord like this, be built up in the ways of God like this. This is the only gift of what is of himself God gives that is just for me, not to be given on to another. One could also think of it in this way. Scripture tells us that it is more blessed to give than to receive; therefore, receiving this gift and using it, wonderful though it is, necessary as it is, it does not compare to those gifts given to us to be spent on others.

Praying in tongues individually requires no interpretation. This is God speaking into me, and out through me, to build me up. Nothing to do with others and, when others do it then it is nothing to do with me, and I do not have to listen avidly, wondering what that means for me. When I pray in tongues, this is one to one with God. However a group of us could agree to all pray in tongues at the same time. At the Centre sometimes, in the midst of worship, we come to a time when we stop singing and all start praying in tongues. We need to practise and practise, and spend seasons in praying in tongues. Read Jackie Pullinger's book *Chasing the Dragon* and discover how, when she prayed in tongues with Chinese drug addicts in Hong Kong, many of them turned to Jesus and were delivered from drug addiction.

When someone speaks in a tongue, the message may be for the congregation, and interpretation is required —vital, in fact. Therefore, when leading a meeting be very aware of this. Often the person who has the interpretation may be too 'shy' to speak out aloud, so do not be afraid to wait awhile. If no one is forthcoming, then as leader you will need to ask the Lord to give you the interpretation before you move on. We need to be aware of that difference between praying and speaking, so that we do not use the gift of tongues inappropriately.

Interpretation
Look up these verses: 1Cor 14:5, 13, 27. As mentioned, interpretation is what is needed when someone has spoken in tongues publicly and so that all may hear, understand and be edified. The gift of interpretation is also employed in explaining

dreams. In both instances we must be subject to the inspiration of the Holy Spirit. Especially in interpreting dreams, we need not to be seduced into using our minds and common sense, or what we have just picked up from the latest pop psychology book or magazine article. You know the sort of thing where things are grouped into categories of meaning: dreaming of houses means one thing; dreaming of water means another. Each person is a unique individual and only the Spirit knows what things are meaningful to them and how. Therefore we should very much lean on the Spirit and seek revelation. Remember that to each one is given the manifestation of the Spirit for the common good. (See 1Corinthians 12:7.)

Prophecy

But everyone who prophesies speaks to men for their strengthening, encouragement and comfort (1Cor14:3). Here we have the New Testament reason for prophesying: to edify or build up, to encourage or exhort, and to comfort.

In the old covenant, before Jesus was incarnate, prophets heard from God and spoke out his word. People would go to them for guidance and direction. Today, in Jesus, each believer can seek the Lord for himself, and this actually is the way we are supposed to do it. The veil was torn in two and the Holy of Holies has become my dwelling place. That is the way one old chorus, using Scripture, describes it. *At that moment the curtain of the temple was torn in two from top to bottom. The earth shook and the rocks split* (Matthew 27:51). We are to seek the King and the kingdom for ourselves, and not go constantly to prophetic people looking for personal words of direction. This is not to deny that someone else may have a prophetic word for us, just that we should not always be seeking others to tell us what the Lord is wanting to say to us. In John10:27, Jesus says, *"My sheep listen to my voice*; I know them, and they follow me. " —so we should follow him, listen to him and obey him. We really should not be investing in others what really belongs to God: our trust and faith in his leading for our lives. So, when praying for others, we can be led by the Holy Spirit to speak words which will encourage them, build them up or comfort them. We should not sit back and say that we are not sure that we hear the Lord. Why not! Why not deal with the uncertainty rather than live with it? Jesus says that we, his sheep hear his voice. If you feel that you do not know or hear the Lord's voice – and it is just a feeling because the truth is that you do hear it and know it – ask him to show you. Then, as the good shepherd that he is, he will come out and get you and show you. Beware of speaking out of soulishness. Wait for the Lord to formulate the words for you, and then you can speak them out. Do not be so swayed by another's sorrow or agony that you rush straight into trying to fix them. That may be your anxiety, your discomfort, or may be touching on unhealed issues in your own life. Wait for the Lord. It is his words which have eternal life not ours.

2. Revelation Gifts

Word of wisdom

To one there is given through the Spirit the message of wisdom, to another the message of knowledge by means of the same Spirit. (1Cor 12:8).

This is usually used to resolve difficult or apparently unanswerable situations. For instance, when Jesus was asked if he would pay taxes (which was a veiled way of saying do you support Rome or us), he answered by showing a coin and asking whose head was on the coin. Upon being told Caesar's, he then answered, *"Give to Caesar what is Caesar's, and to*

God what is God's" (Matthew 22:21). In the Old Testament we are given a very good example of the kind of wisdom we are looking at when Solomon gave the decision on which of the women should have the baby.

You may be told of a very difficult situation and be asked to give your opinion or solution. Beware! And be aware that this is where you need the Holy Spirit to reveal the word of wisdom appropriate to that situation. What is not needed is your opinion, or your solution, or indeed your assessment. Do not be seduced into trying to sort it all out. Only do what the Lord shows you to do, and only say what the Lord tells you to say. If he shows you nothing, then do nothing; if he tells you nothing, then say nothing.

Word of knowledge

To one there is given through the Spirit the message of wisdom, to another the message of knowledge by means of the same Spirit (1 Corinthians 12:8). This concerns things revealed by the Holy Spirit of which you could have NO knowledge. It will speak volumes to your hearer, and usually will mean little or nothing to you. Indeed, this gift is sometimes very difficult to grow in, as we may believe that what has come into our minds is so trivial, or unrelated to what they have come about, that we can dismiss it out of hand or overlook it. For instance, someone may have a broken leg, and all you have is a picture of swans landing on a lake. That might seem a crazy thing to tell them. Remember if you have committed yourself to serve the Lord, he will give whatever is needed in that situation. He will make you aware and will give you ways of saying it. You can offer what you are aware of like this: 'I have a strong sense/a picture of/a feeling of... a place of peace, or a swan gliding on a lake (or whatever it is) and then say, 'Is this significant for you?' Usually it is. Remember that God trains and encourages us!

As an example— a lady came to me with a neck and back problem, but all I had was a picture in my mind of a snowy night, and I told her so. It turned out that it was on such a night that the neck and back problem had started. She had received a shock when some snow fell off a roof on to her. I spoke into the trauma of that night which was still holding her in shock, and told it go —and set her free. Her neck and back problem were immediately released and the pain left.

Discernment of spirits

After this, Jesus traveled about from one town and village to another, proclaiming the good news of the kingdom of God. The Twelve were with him (Luke 8:1f). *At that very time Jesus cured many who had diseases, sicknesses and evil spirits, and gave sight to many who were blind* (Luke 7:21).

This is something we can expect to come up against as we ask the Holy Spirit to lead us into the truth. If you are praying for others, it is important to be well prepared. Preparation beforehand will equip you to be a clear channel of this particular gifting. Be sure you are clear to pray with no unforgiveness, bitterness or outstanding agenda. Any of these things cloud our vision, and the things of darkness can hide with ease around us where we are in darkness. So come walking in the light of God, cleared up to that point of any known sin. Do not engage in conversation with any demonic presence you become aware of. Resist it, and it will flee from you. As the Holy Spirit directs, you can pronounce cleansing prayers or words of command, but definitely do not engage in conversation. Be sensitive in your use of language. The person you are praying for may be terrified at the thought of having a demon, or knowing they are around them, and I repeat, follow the leading of the Spirit in your use of language and communication of what he gives you.

3. Gifts of power

Faith

For by the grace given me I say to every one of you: Do not think of yourself more highly than you ought, but rather think of yourself with sober judgment, in accordance with the measure of faith God has given you (Romans 12:3). Each person has a measure of faith, and it is this we move in at all times because without it is impossible to please God. But the *gift* of faith is one given for specific times or occasions. With it, we can claim on behalf of the other person the provision the Lord has just shown. This gift manifests itself in an 'I know that I know that I know' type of way. The certainty not that it will be done but that it has been done is just so concrete that there are no questions in your mind or heart. It is established.

Miracles

These come along in the course of the ways of praying that we have been discussing. They are distinctive, not always instantaneous, but absolutely only in God's power to do —such as the changing of wine into water; walking on water; feeding five thousand, etc., in Jesus' ministry.

Healings

We see a lot of these at the Centre, small and large, tender and amazing, often in conjunction with the other gifts mentioned before.

The source of spiritual gifts

For in Christ all the fullness of the Deity dwells in bodily form, and you have been given fullness in Christ (Col 2:9).

God is the source of the 'gifts'. He is the giver. Jesus Christ, true God and true man, promised the coming of the Holy Spirit, and he, God the Holy Spirit, gives the gifts, which are always to be exercised in love. Finally, *And over all these virtues put on love, which binds them all together in perfect unity* (Col 3:14). *If I speak in the tongues of men and of angels, but have not love, I am only a resounding gong or a clanging cymbal* (1Cor 13:1). When we think of the giftings of the Holy Spirit, we always remember that God is love. If we try to move in any of the gifts without him, we are like a clanging gong and we miss the mark.

1 Corinthians 12	Shows us the gifts of the Spirit
Ephesians 4	... of the Son
Romans 12:6–8	... of the Father

Never forget this truth: that the gifts are given by God himself. Let us learn to be able workmen with his word, and approach him with reverence and awe. We 'use' the spiritual gifts with gratitude to him, in his service, constantly aware that we need the grace and infilling of his Holy Spirit, the giver. He alone makes it all possible; he works effectually, and we are aware of his indwelling presence and his life, as we use the gifts in the way we have been taught in Scripture to do —in his love, filled with that same Spirit. We see fruit flowing from the right exercise of spiritual gifts. We see and are encouraged by the effects of his actions in edifying, building up, equipping, healing, confirming his proclaimed word in signs and wonders.

MODULE 5

THE CYCLE OF GRACE

Much of the following material is taken from Learning to Listen *which is one of the many* Listening *training courses provided by the Acorn Christian Healing Foundation. For information about their training courses and resources please look them up at their website address* www.acornchristian.org

Start by getting the people present to split into pairs. Preferably they should choose a partner whom they know little about. Ask them to listen – just listen; no commenting – to each other for two minutes each. In that two minutes they are just to say something which they feel is relevant about themselves at this time. Then they are each in one minute to reflect back to the other what they have learned about them. Make sure that they change over at the two minute and one minute points for reflections.

Gather the whole group together. Ask whether they feel that they were fully listened to and truly heard. Ask them to cast their minds back over the past week (not counting this session) and consider whether they feel that they have been listened to in a way that was meaningful to them when they

needed it. Ask those who feel they have to raise their hands.
For the remainder, ask them next to consider back over the
past year. Then for the rest: have they ever really felt heard?
You may well find someone who has never felt they have been
listened to and heard.

Ask how many have been listeners for someone else in the
same way?

Dr Frank Lake founded the Clinical Theology Association,
which is now the Bridge Pastoral Foundation. Very briefly, as
I understand it, 'clinical theology' involves recognising the
effects that various events in the past, even preconception, can
have on the 'health' of a person throughout their life. I gather
that his initial consideration was that inner healing – emotional,
mental – could be initiated by encouraging the client to envisage
Jesus with them in the past situation. Much of the teaching on
inner and emotional healing that I have heard and read from
others is structured around such understanding. However I have
been informed by a reputable source that before he died (in 1982
Lake) changed his way of thinking and practice and moved to
the model which is used in this Centre. This change had nothing
to do with us. The Centre did not exist in 1982. Again very
briefly – rather than delving into times past – we rely on the
Holy Spirit to highlight some event or situation for the client
and then bring this to Jesus in the light of the kingdom now,
where it can be fully healed. Jesus is alive today —the healing
was won on the cross and is to be appropriated today.

Lake, and Emil Brunner, a Swiss theologian, were trying to
find a model for people to live by through which they could
live a completely balanced and resourced life. They realised
that this could only be modelled on a perfect person. The only
perfect man they knew about was and is Jesus, so they examined
aspects of his life and, from that, devised a model. They called
this model the 'dynamic cycle', but I like to think about it as

the 'cycle of grace' because everything should flow out from and through God's grace to us.

In some way or other we are all called into a life of service. Constantly, all kinds of conflicting demands are being forced upon us. This is especially true in the lives of those who are involved in caring professions or caring roles. This must include raising families and running homes. We need to know how we can do this without constantly finding ourselves drained flat like batteries, and worn out.

One of the great dangers for carers is that of empathy. Empathy is taught in many schools of counselling as being the best way of understanding and befriending the client but just look at what Collins English Dictionary says. "Empathy; the power of understanding and imaginatively entering into another person's feelings. See also 'identification' (sense 3b). Identification 3b; – the process by one which incorporates aspects of another person's personality.

It is not incumbent upon us to enter into any other person's feelings. Appreciate and understand yes, but enter in? No. Nor should we incorporate any aspect of another person's personality. In fact it is wrong and dangerous. God made us each as an individual personality —he gave us free will, and the only one we should allow to have any hand in changing that is Father himself. With empathy we are in fact endeavouring to take the place of Jesus. On the cross Jesus took into himself all sickness and sin —it is not for us to try to do it for him. Before he died on the cross, when he walked this earth as a man anointed in the Holy Spirit (Luke 4) it tells us that he was full of compassion and showed compassion —he did not empathise with the person and become part of the problem. Compassion is a feeling of distress and pity for the suffering or misfortune of another, often including the desire to alleviate it. Jesus stood outside the person and brought them into healing.

Lake and Brunner looked at Jesus in his three years of ministry. Just think of all that happened in those three years; and, as we are told, just a tiny fraction of all that happened and what he did is recorded. Yet he seemed to do everything calmly and 'matter-of-factly' with a complete sense of order and peace and trust around him.

Get the class to suggest some such events. They could include such as this, for example: when they were going to stone him — he walked quietly through their midst; or arrest him — he stood and waited whilst they picked themselves up. On the cross he took the time to think of others — including his mother's future. From all the stories emanates a profound trust in Father. How do we do this? Use overhead of diagram. Cover up all of the diagram except Acceptance.

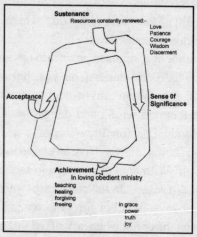

This is basically all about unconditional acceptance and how we need to know that we are unconditionally accepted by Father God, and have this understanding written deep, deep into our very being, just as Jesus did. See Luke 3:22, *and the Holy Spirit descended on him in bodily form like a dove. And a voice came from heaven: "You are my Son, whom I love; with you I am well pleased."*

Do you know that you are God's beloved son and that he is well pleased with you?

We started the session with a brief exercise on listening and thinking back to the times when we considered we were heard, or we realised that we have never felt heard. When you pray or talk to God and tell him things? Do you expect him to hear and expect him to reply? Jesus did. *So they took away the stone. Then Jesus looked up and said, "Father, I thank you that you have heard me. I knew that you always hear me..."* (John 11:41f). Jesus knew that he was not only always heard but always had been heard. (Maybe give examples from your own life.)

Uncover Sustenance

Do you know that all that you ever need or will need to keep you sustained can and will be supplied by Father God if we can come to a place of being totally trusting and reliant on him? — *If you remain in me and my words remain in you, ask whatever you wish, and it will be given you* (John 15:7). Whenever Jesus was under pressure or had decisions to make, before he did anything he went to Father God. Before he was to make the momentous decision that was to have an everlasting effect on the world, the decision to choose the disciples, he was under attack from the Pharisees. He did not draw up a 'Disciple Profile'; he did not write a job description; he did not advertise and ask for CVs, then draw up a shortlist after interview. No, he went and spent the night with the Father and then came down and announced his decisions. He and his Father decided together. He got all the wisdom and insight that he needed. *One of those days Jesus went out to a mountainside to pray, and spent the night praying to God. When morning came, he called his disciples to him and chose twelve of them, whom he also designated apostles: Simon (whom he named Peter), his brother Andrew, James, John, Philip, Bartholomew, Matthew, Thomas, James son of Alphaeus, Simon who was called the Zealot, Judas son of James, and Judas Iscariot, who became a traitor* (Luke 6:12–16). If he needed anything – wisdom, courage, strength, discernment – he went to the Father and knew he would receive. As he said to the disciples, *"So I say to you: Ask and it will be given to you; seek and you will find; knock and the door will be opened to you"* (Luke 11:9).

Uncover Significance

Jesus had no doubts about who he was. He knew who he was. He knew who 'I am' was, and all of this flowed out from the fact that he knew he was unconditionally loved. *Then Jesus declared, "I am the bread of life. He who comes to me will never go hungry, and he who believes in me will never be thirsty* (John 6:35). *Therefore Jesus said again, "I tell you the truth, I am the gate for the sheep* (John 10:7). *"I am the good shepherd. The good shepherd lays down his life for the sheep"* (John 10:11). *Jesus said to her, "I am the resurrection and the life. He who believes in me will live, even though he dies* (John 11:25). *Jesus answered, "I am the way and the truth and the life. No one comes to the Father except through me"* (John 14:6). *"I am the vine; you are the branches. If a man remains in me and I in him, he will bear much fruit; apart from me you can do nothing"* (John 15:5). Do you know that this also works for you? It does, because— *In this way, love is made complete among us so that we will have confidence on the day of judgment, because in this world we are like him* (1 John 4:17). I prefer the AV/KJV version of the end of this verse because it spells it out more emphatically and leaves us without doubt of the totality of our likeness to him. It translates as: *because as he is, so also are we in this world.*

Do you know some of the 'I ams' that became possible for us

when we were born again? Such as these:

I am born again to a living hope. (See 1 Peter 1:3.)

I am protected by the power of God. (See 1 Peter 1:5.)

I am a son of God. (See John 1:12.)

I am an overcomer. (See 1 John 5:5.)

I am a saint. (See Ephesians 2:19.)

Ask the people to think of more scriptural 'I ams', and exhort them to think of them and use them to encourage themselves every day.

Uncover Achievement

So many of us get completely worn out trying to prove that we are worthwhile by all the things that we do and have done. But do we ask Father first whether he wants us to do this? Remember the work of the Father is that we believe that he whom he sent is the Son of God. That's it. That is the work that we are instructed to do. Then, if we do that, everything else will just flow out from it.

Jesus only did the Father's work. He told us he only did what he saw the Father do and said what he heard the Father say. Achievement for Jesus was not to do what he thought people needed or wanted of him, or what would make him popular —he only did what the Father asked. He was in total obedience. Ask the class to name some of the things that Jesus did and then uncover them on the overhead. He—

Preached the kingdom

Healed

Taught

Forgave

Set free

Raised the dead

Deliverance

Jesus did all these things in dependence on the Father. All

things flowed from the starting point of being accepted, and the achievements flowed from this, not the other way round. He was not acceptable to Father because of all that he did and achieved. No, it was because he knew he was acceptable to Father that all these things flowed out from him. This is the flow of the dynamic cycle. Always refreshed, always sustained, always sure of his ground and who he was, whether they were trying to kill him or lock him up as a lunatic (remember his family wanted to do this).

Christianity is not religion. Christianity is our relationship with Father, Son and Holy Spirit. The son of a friend of mine once said, "Religion will not change the world; relationship will." The first reference to God in the Bible in the first verse of the first chapter of Genesis is as *Elohim*, which means plurality in unity —referring to the three in one, and the fellowship and relationship of Father, Son and Holy Spirit. To spend some uninterrupted time with the Father, we know that Jesus went into the hills. Ask the class about the ways that they find enable them to come closer in a relationship with Father, which bring them strength and peace. (E.g. hills, flowers, snowy days, birdsong, being with family or friends, during times of prayer or in the midst of worship, whether with others or alone, etc.) How many of us are fully aware that in Jesus we have the opportunity to receive and know the acceptance, the sustenance, the significance of who we are and then let the achievements flow out from this?

Now take FRUSTRATION and place it on top of the cycle from achievement. You will see that it is going in the opposite direction to the flow of grace. Instead of a dynamic cycle we tend to work in a cycle of frustration because we go the wrong way round. We are always trying to prove that we are worthwhile and worthy because of what we have done.

At this point, perhaps use an illustration of your own. For instance, I may tell of how I left school at the age of sixteen, with seven GCSEs —but against my father's wish for me to stay on and go to university and get that piece of paper which would be the entrance to everything worthwhile, and without which he said I would be of no significance. I said I would show him and achieve without it. I then chased pieces of paper— banker's exams; chartered secretaries; Civil Service Examination in Mandarin Chinese; Fellow of the Institute of Marketing; Fellow of the Institute of Directors; General Ordination Certificate; priesting; MA. And so on. Who was I? Who am I? Father God showed me with a stick of candy rock. He gave me a picture of a stick of candy rock, and written right through it was not the name of a seaside resort, as is normal, but my name. Right through the rock were the words 'Randolph, son of God'. He was saying to me that this was who I was —right though me. Like the stick of rock – if it got broken in pieces; if it got crushed; if it got licked – it would still say 'Randolph, son of God' right through it.

Ask the class to think about how they reply when someone asks whether or not they have had a good day. Ask various members whether they have had a good day. Check on the replies and see how many answer on the lines of: 'Not very good; I did not get much done —or, 'Great, I managed to do so and so, and so and so....' From the replies you should be able to demonstrate how often we are more aware of what we are doing rather than who we are being. Dorothy always says that God made 'beings', not 'doings'.

Look at some of the reasons that may be stopping us from fully knowing our acceptability to God. Go through some with the class; get them to think about and then comment on situations such as: fear of rejection, and experiences of not being acceptable or worthwhile. E.g. —

Nothing they did reached mum or dad's standards or

requirements of you.

Not wanted at home.

Wallflower at a dance.

Not picked for teams: football, netball, etc.

Too fat or the wrong shape or physique for PE.

Not clever enough to pass exams.

Not able to get the job they wanted.

[Guide them with the use case studies of people you have worked with. Such as the lady I mention I my book. (The Anointing to Heal, chapter 6, pp 110–112). Her twin brother died in the womb alongside her. Her parents already had two girls and wanted a boy. So when she was born and her brother was stillborn, her parents rejected her – would not even name her – she grew up every day never knowing a day when she did not wish she was dead.]

Passed over at work.

Made redundant.

'Big boys don't cry.'

'Now you are the man of the house.'

'All girls should be able to sew, cook, and bake.'

Turn the frustration acetate over, and show how we should flow. Depending on time, get the class to ask questions about any point of which they are not sure. Then think about and comment on any particular point of the session that was especially meaningful to them.

We need to flow dynamically, always knowing that we are unconditionally acceptable to God, and therefore he will sustain us in everything. We are significant purely and simply because he loves us and accepts us. All our achievements flow in loving obedience to him.

MODULE 6

MODELS OF MINISTRY

Introduction

It is absolutely necessary to read and teach this module with reference to the book *The Anointing to Heal*. The theology behind many of the practical applications referred to, and the reasons and the methods of using them, are detailed in the book. Also there is need to make reference to most of the other modules.

This is the most difficult chapter and module to write because it is an outline of the practical application of all the other modules put together. To properly cover the material in a two and a half-hour session, and include practical demonstration, is really impossible. Therefore, in a two and a half-hour session the leader can only employ teaching and discussion. In order to include practical demonstration and the physical application of some of the models, we expand it to a full day. Even on a full day the delegates usually say that it would be good to have a week to practise all that we would want to suggest.

The objective of the this section is to enable a team to minister in the context of a public service where the ministry takes place in front of the assembly. These are not suggestions for counselling or one to one ministry in private sessions. Because all that takes place is in full view of the congregation it will be seen that greater flexibility in approach is possible.

This is about 'how do we do it?' E.g. 'How and when do we lay on hands?' 'How do we heal?' At this we can relax a little because we only lay on hands and Jesus does the healing. We are not healers – Jesus is the healer. We can think of ourselves as agents in his process of healing when we allow our hands to be used. We do not heal anyone —Jesus does. We make ourselves available. I am repeating myself to stress the importance of this concept. There is no place in this ministry for self or pride. (See Cycle of Grace – Module 5.) When we realise this, then it takes the pressure off us. The question is more: How can we be useful without getting in the way?

Section 1

Ask the delegates to write down as many methods of ministry as they can think of, and also indicate whether they are familiar with using them. Model, e.g. , 'laying on of hands' — I use/don't use, etc.

When they have listed as many as they can, ask them to call out their answers and write them up on a paper or blackboard. You will get examples such as those in this a-z list. However they will probably not mention all of these at this stage, therefore only write up those, which they do suggest and leave the remainder until later in the session.

Laying on hands.

Deliverance – casting out.

Touching

Being touched

Rebuking

Deliverance

Anointing

Distant healing (proxy or cloths etc)
Forgiveness – of others, of self, of God – Honour your father and your mother...
Holding (in love)
Spitting
Listening to the person
Listening to God
Prophetic
Words of knowledge and/or wisdom, etc
Tongues
Prayer
Praise
Speaking to the problem
Communion
Kneeling down and being prayed over.
First the blood and then the oil.
Cutting of soul ties and spiritual ties.
Cutting of generational ties.
Release from genetic conditions.
Release from vows and curses.

There are many ways of ministering the healing of Jesus to the sick, and we may need to try a number of methods before we see someone move into their healing. Strangely enough there are no examples in the Bible of Jesus or the disciples actually *praying for* healing for the sick as they ministered to them. Prayer is to Father God to know his will. Nor is prayer to sickness. Jesus and the disciples prayed to God first, to know his will, and then they acted and dealt with the problem. As we know, it is the nature and will of God to heal, and we do not pray to ask him to heal them 'if it is his will'. We do need to pray to him and listen to how he wants us to proceed, and if there are things about the situation which he wants to reveal to us. We need to spend seasons in prayer if we are to work in this ministry. Nor are there any examples of getting the sick to kneel down and then lay hands on their heads, although for some reason this has become the most popular model used in churches. There are however many examples and exhortations in the Scriptures that we should lay hands on the sick, but these are usually appropriate to the condition. Distressed babies are comforted as they are touched, held or stroked, and this can largely also be related to distressed adults.

Nor are there any scriptural examples of the sick being offered communion directly in relation to healing. Again this has become one of the major methods used in many denominations. Obviously, before the last supper and the death and resurrection of Jesus one would not expect to see this, but in Acts and the epistles it would have been available but is not described.

However, this is not to say that to use any such method, even though it is not described in the Scriptures, is a wrong thing to do. A number of the methods we offer are not directly drawn from scriptural example, but through experience we have found them to be efficacious.

Here is a sample of the many models of ministry that we find in the Scriptures.

Give out the 'hand out notes', which do not have the headings against each letter. Divide the delegates into groups, giving each group a section of the Scripture verses, and ask them to decide which method is being employed and write in against the letter. Give them 15 minutes to make their decisions, then bring them back into plenary session to discuss and compare what they have concluded, with the suggested headings given here. Then compare these with the list previously written up. Again, there is no definite right or wrong answer.

(a) Lay on hands
"...they will place their hands on sick people, and they will get well" (Mark 16:18).

(b) Rebuke
So he bent over her and rebuked the fever, and it left her. She got up at once and began to wait on them (Luke 4:39)

(c) Touch
Filled with compassion, Jesus reached out his hand and touched the man. "I am willing," he said. "Be clean!" (Mark 1:41)

(d) Speak
He took her by the hand and said to her, "Talitha koum!" (which means, "Little girl, I say to you, get up!") (Mark 5:41)

(e) Touch and spit and speak (Spitting is probably not a good idea in our culture.)
After he took him aside, away from the crowd, Jesus put his fingers into the man's ears. Then he spit and touched the man's tongue. He looked up to heaven and with a deep sigh said to him, "Ephphatha!" (which means, "Be opened!"). (Mark 7:33f).

(f) Speak and believe
"I tell you the truth, if anyone says to this mountain, 'Go, throw yourself into the sea,' and does not doubt in his heart but believes that what he says will happen, it will be done for him. Therefore I tell you, whatever you ask for in prayer, believe that you have received it, and it will be yours" (Mark 11:23f).

(g) Forgive
"And when you stand praying, if you hold anything against anyone, forgive him, so that your Father in heaven may forgive you your sins. But if you do not forgive, neither will your Father who is in heaven forgive your sins" (Mark 11:25f).

(h) Command faith into action
He looked around at them in anger and, deeply distressed at their stubborn hearts, said to the man, "Stretch out your hand." He stretched it out, and his hand was completely restored.

(Mark 3:5). *Then Jesus said to him, "Get up! Pick up your mat and walk"* (John 5:8). *"Go," he told him, "wash in the Pool of Siloam" (this word means Sent). So the man went and washed, and came home seeing* (John 9:7).

(i) Anoint with saliva and clay

Having said this, he spit on the ground, made some mud with the saliva, and put it on the man's eyes (John 9:6).

(j) Let the sick touch you

...and the people all tried to touch him, because power was coming from him and healing them all (Luke 6:19).

And wherever he went—into villages, towns or countryside— they placed the sick in the marketplaces. They begged him to let them touch even the edge of his cloak, and all who touched him were healed (Mark 6:56).

When she heard about Jesus, she came up behind him in the crowd and touched his cloak, because she thought, "If I just touch his clothes, I will be healed" (Mark 5:27f).

(k) Anointed cloths

God did extraordinary miracles through Paul, so that even handkerchiefs and aprons that had touched him were taken to the sick, and their illnesses were cured and the evil spirits left them (Acts 19:11f).

(l) Deliverance

When Jesus saw that a crowd was running to the scene, he rebuked the evil spirit. "You deaf and mute spirit," he said, "I command you, come out of him and never enter him again." The spirit shrieked, convulsed him violently and came out. The boy looked so much like a corpse that many said, "He's dead" (Mark 9:25f).

(m) Take the authority over sickness and cast out demons

He called his twelve disciples to him and gave them authority to drive out evil spirits and to heal every disease and sickness (Matthew 10:1).

When Jesus had called the Twelve together, he gave them power and authority to drive out all demons and to cure diseases (Luke 9:1).

(n) Deliver and anoint

They drove out many demons and anointed many sick people with oil and healed them (Mark 6:13).

(o) Forgiveness

When they could not find a way to do this because of the crowd, they went up on the roof and lowered him on his mat through the tiles into the middle of the crowd, right in front of Jesus. When Jesus saw their faith, he said, "Friend, your sins are forgiven" (Luke 5:19f).

(p) Speak faith

"Go," said Jesus, "your faith has healed you." Immediately he received his sight and followed Jesus along the road (Mark 10:52).

(q) Gradual healing and spitting

They came to Bethsaida, and some people brought a blind man and begged Jesus to touch him. He took the blind man by the hand and led him outside the village. When he had spit on the man's eyes and put his hands on him, Jesus asked, "Do you see anything?" He looked up and said, "I see people; they look like trees walking around." Once more Jesus put his hands on the man's eyes. Then his eyes were opened, his sight was restored, and he saw everything clearly (Mark 8:22ff).

(r) Absent healing

Once more he visited Cana in Galilee, where he had turned the water into wine. And there was a certain royal official whose son lay sick at Capernaum. When this man heard that Jesus had arrived in Galilee from Judea, he went to him and begged him to come and heal his son, who was close to death.

"Unless you people see miraculous signs and wonders," Jesus told him, "you will never believe."

The royal official said, "Sir, come down before my child dies."

Jesus replied, "You may go. Your son will live."

The man took Jesus at his word and departed. While he was still on the way, his servants met him with the news that his boy was living. When he inquired as to the time when his son got better, they said to him, "The fever left him yesterday at the seventh hour." Then the father realised that this was the exact time at which Jesus had said to him, "Your son will live." So he and all his household believed (John 4:46ff).

(s) Gifts

...to another faith by the same Spirit, to another gifts of healing by that one Spirit (1 Corinthians 12:9).

(t) Eldership and anointing

Is any one of you sick? He should call the elders of the church to pray over him and anoint him with oil in the name of the Lord (James 5:14). *And the prayer offered in faith will make the sick person well; the Lord will raise him up. If he has sinned, he will be forgiven* (James 5:15).

Section 2 Practicalities of ministering

Before a healing service

As we stress in Module 7 (Be clear for prayer), we need to be sure that we are in the right place with the Lord and that we and all who will come to the service will be safe. Therefore before every service the ministry team meet together for prayer. We each personally need to repent and be forgiven and to ask the Lord to show us any place of unforgiveness within us —and then do something about it. Whoever is leading the prayer time will cover the following points:

Cleanse themselves and the team with repentance and invoke the blood of Christ.

Cleanse the building and the meeting room and plead the blood of Jesus.

Plead the blood on the exits and the entrances of the building and the grounds.

Ask the Lord to post his angels to guard the doors so that nothing of the enemy can enter in to harm anyone.

Ask him to post angels at the gates.

Ask him to post angels along the roads to keep everyone safe and they come to and go from the meeting.

Ask God to remind all those who need to come but have been dithering.

Ask for gifts of wisdom, discernment and healing – in fact for all the gifts that the team might need during proceedings, and pray that they will be open to hear and to receive.

Ask Jesus to cover everyone – the team, the visitors, etc – and to guard them so that nothing of the enemy or from anyone else can stick to them or enter them and go out from the meeting with them. I call this the 'Holy Spirit non stick Teflon coated prayer'.

Ask the Father and Jesus to be present in glory, and the power of the Holy Spirit to fill the place.

Pray for those leading the worship.

Pray for those speaking.

Pray for the ministry team.

Ask for words of knowledge. (We write these down and give them out to the meeting before the ministry time.)

We normally finish with a prayer such as St. Patrick's Breastplate:

Christ be with me, Christ within me,
Christ behind me, Christ before me,
Christ beside me, Christ to win me,
Christ to comfort and restore me,
Christ beneath me, Christ above me,
Christ in quiet, Christ in danger,
Christ in hearts of all that love me,
Christ in mouth of friend or stranger.
I bind unto myself the Name,
The strong name of the Trinity,
By invocation of the same,
The Three in One and the One in Three,
Of whom all nature hath creation,
Eternal Father, Spirit, Word:
Salvation is of Christ the Lord.
Praise to the Lord of my salvation,

Self assessment and practical application

In this section we raise practical questions that the class need to be able to answer. Have them discuss these and others that may arise during discussion. Given time, have them practise some of the models on each other, and expect to see healing. For instance, to practise aligning the skeleton it is good to start with someone who has back pain. Make sure there is sufficient space and adequately soft flooring for you to demonstrate, and for the students to practise with each other.

Catching

Do you know how to catch safely? (The catcher, by gently touching the back of the client lets them know that there is someone in place to assist. The catcher needs to stand sufficiently close to the client so that their fall does not gain any momentum before the catcher intervenes. The catcher should hold the client under the elbows and lower them backwards to the floor —if necessary sliding them down the catcher's body to take the weight and slow the rate of descent.)

To stand or to sit —does it matter?

If the client is physically incapable of standing, then there is no option. However we encourage anyone wanting ministry to get up from the chair and come to the front, where the prayer ministers are standing. As they walk forward, they are walking into their healing. Their decision to come to the meeting started them into the process of receiving their healing; this has continued through the journey to the meeting; the praise, worship and hearing the word have added to this, and now they are putting their faith into action by coming forward to receive. We get many requests from people for us to visit them or to see them privately. Unless we know something particular about a situation, we always urge them to come to our regular Thursday healing service and promise we will discuss their situation and further needs following the service. Experience has shown us that in the environment of the corporate power of Christians gathered together in worship the reception of healing – emotional, physical or spiritual – is greater and faster and deeper than that which is normally possible in one to one counselling situations. We have witnessed emotional and spiritual healing from years and years of inner hurts, that would have taken two or three years of counselling to unravel, dealt with in five or ten minutes of Holy Spirit ministry.

Gender to gender

Should it be same sex ministry always? Sometimes? Never?

Points to consider

Normally in the context of an open meeting there really isn't a problem. However, some people, both men and women, may have been abused and find difficulty, so we should not force people to have to go to any one minister — let them choose. At the Centre we usually have the possibility of all the combinations: man and woman; man and man; woman and man; even one to one —but all in view.

To hug or not to hug; to hold or not to hold

Is hugging appropriate? When? When is it not? *The Anointing to Heal* check pages 9–10; 15; 81–84; Pat Scovell's story, 47–52.

Points to consider

Maybe the person has been abused, and the thought of being hugged by a man will have them running away, not coming to receive ministry. Some people may find their attention drawn to the minister, not to Jesus. Sometimes, people need to feel the arms of Jesus around them. If in doubt, don't —especially male to female. But remember, we are talking about ministering in an open forum, so there is less likelihood of cries of inappropriate behaviour being made. It is possible to stand to welcome the person with arms slightly open, so that they can initiate the hug if they wish.

Touching

Should you touch or avoid touching? When is it good to touch and is it ever wrong to?

Points to consider

Appropriate touch is good and healthy, but can be frightening for some. Touch should be gentle and light, but not so light as to be ticklish. Any touch should never be forceful. (Smith Wigglesworth punched someone hard in the stomach who had cancer, but that would not be legally permissible today!)

Don't push people over to make yourself feel successful. Offering touch when people come forward, but not requiring it, is welcoming without being threatening.

Volume and sensitivity
How loudly should you talk to the client?

Points to consider
Speak loudly enough that they can hear clearly without straining. If they are straining, try to speak quietly enough so that confidentiality is maintained. Worship, especially live worship, if at all possible should continue quietly during ministry. This then covers the conversations.

Confidentiality and supervision
Should you share the problem with another if you feel stuck? And with whom should you share?

Points to consider
If you are stuck, you could say to the person that you are going to get someone else to help pray – is that alright? If you have a problem yourself afterwards, then take it to the person in charge of the meeting. You need to get difficulties sorted out that you have had raised in you and those in authority, for the meeting/group, etc., are there for you as much as for those coming for prayer. Do not take the details of a ministry time to anyone else —people require and deserve confidentiality.

Medication considerations and doctors

Points to consider

What should you do if someone asks if they should continue taking their medicine if they feel healed? You can tell them to keep taking the medication and seek their doctor's advice. You can pray that the medication will have no harmful effects until it is discontinued.

Modesty cloths

What are they for and when do you use them?

Points to consider

Appropriately sized cloths should be available to cover any exposed areas.

Tears and hankies

Are you comfortable when people get upset? Does it bother you? What do you think is the best way to handle this?

Points to consider

Why do you get upset? Is this touching on a part of your own hurt? Module 7 touches on this. Don't try to get people to stop crying. Find the hankies and let them be free to express whatever is within. If you know they are crocodile tears designed for attention seeking, then quietly, and/or in tongues, speak to the situation, and tell the person to be quiet. Have a supply of tissues available.

Should you show emotions ever when ministering?

Points to consider

Sometimes God seems to give us feelings —the same physical

or emotional pain. The person needs to know that we are still okay, so we may start crying, but the tears should never overtake us; we should allow them, but still be available for Holy Spirit to speak to and minister through us.

Anointing with oil

See Pat Hardy's story in *The Anointing to Heal* pp 175–182.

Points to consider

First the blood and then the oil. Do you know how to do this? Would you feel comfortable if you had to do it right now. What kind of oil? Different churchmanship equals different methods, e.g. Anglican/Catholic = Using an oil stock and simply signing with the cross on the forehead or hands, etc. Pentecostal = Bottle of oil from which the minister pours oil into his hand and smears it on the supplicant (this oil is often perfumed). Do not allow any fluid to drip down on to eyes. Some of the perfumed oils have additives. Be sure no potential irritant is an ingredient.

Prophetic: see *The Anointing to Heal*, chapter 6.

Distant healing —proxy: see *The Anointing to Heal*, p 183.

Forgiveness/honour father and mother: see *The Anointing to Heal* pp 126, 130–132, 165–166; Module 7 (Be Clear for Prayer); Module 6 (Cycle of Grace).

To pray or to talk?

Points to consider

Should you always pray over the person?

Or should you sometimes counsel the person?

Do you know how to tell the difference?

Do you feel comfortable not praying?

Avoid 'nice' prayers.

This is dealt with in Listening to God (5) and Listening to Others (4).

Tongues or English?

Do you know which to use and when and why?

Points to consider

English if you want the person's mind to understand.

Tongues if you are having difficulty in hearing God.

Tongues if you feel you want to speak to the condition and by-pass the person's intellectual understanding.

Deliverance

Do you know how to go about this or are you not sure? See *The Anointing to Heal* pp 90–95.

Points to consider

If you're not sure, then best advice is get someone who does. See Module 2 (Knowing your authority).

Aligning the skeleton

Do you know how to pray about leg lengthening, back straightening and so on? See Pat's story in *The Anointing to Heal* pp 47–54, 25–28,

Curses, vows, soul ties, generational issues

Do you know how to minister? See *The Anointing to Heal* chapter 8, pp 133f.

Points to consider

See Module 7 (Be Clear for Prayer) and Module 8 (Cycle of Grace).

Allergies, fears, phobias and depression

Do you know how to minister in these? See *The Anointing to Heal* chapter 9 and pp 90–95.

Points to consider

It is often important to find the root cause. Basically, you are coming against soulish strongholds, or even brokenness in the Spirit, and these need to be broken down.

Do you need to understand the medical condition?

Points to consider

Sometimes it gets in the way. It can cause doubt in your own heart. You can be tempted to invent prayers to suit what you know, rather than listen to God to see how he wants to proceed.

Is it important if the person is saved or not? Do you need to know this?

Points to consider

They do not have to be saved to get healed. Even before Jesus died and rose again, people were getting healed. However, salvation is of paramount importance to eternal life, so we should always ensure that we give them the opportunity to ask Jesus to be Lord of their life

Is it important that the person is baptised in the Spirit? Do you need to know this?

Points to consider

Purely in terms of receiving healing, it is not a prerequisite. But it is, of course, to be commended, and at appropriate moments help can be given to receive all that the Lord wills to impart, with the use of appropriate passages of Scripture.

"This person has so many problems, where do I start?" How should this situation be handled?

Points to consider
One problem at a time! Remember, you are not the answer to their problem, Jesus is. The Holy Spirit is your source of information on how to deal with the situation, not the knowledge you have amassed over the years. See particularly Module 7 (Be clear for Prayer) and 8 (Listening to God).

Personal hygiene. Is it important? Why/why not?
It is very important. We do not want anything about us getting in the way of the person we are ministering to. Deodorant– fresh breath – perfume/afershave (but not so strongly that we can smell you coming fifty paces before you walk in the door. That is the opposite of the body odour problem!)

Last, but not least—
Be sure that any statutory requirements which may be in place for the protection of those involved in personal ministry have been complied with. (In the United Kingdom this may include criminal record checks. Denominational offices should be able to provide helpful information about current requirements.)

MODULE 7

BE CLEAR FOR PRAYER

1. Effective prayer needs:

A Christian
The Word
The power of the Holy Spirit at work in us

If we are interceding, we have to know God's conditions before we come before the throne of grace. Before we start to pray we need to know that we are praying the Father's will and can expect to receive the manifestation and fulfilment of our petition. With regard to the ministry of healing, therefore, we must be very sure we understand the nature and will of God to heal (see Module 1). When praying in relation to healing we should not add the rider 'if it is your will'. Using such a phrase is not showing humility. Not using such a phrase is not being presumptuous, because God's will in the matter has already been revealed.

Ask if anyone knows any passage in the Scriptures in which Jesus or a disciple prays for healing.

I have not found one passage in the New Testament where Jesus or a disciple prays for healing. There are numerous passages where they pray to God the Father before they minister in healing, but none where they pray for the healing. This is not splitting hairs. Prayer is to and with Father God; we speak to the situation. When asked how they should pray, Jesus told them in Matthew 6:9, "This, then, is how you should pray: "'Our Father in heaven, hallowed be your name.....'"

I repeat: prayer is to God. We speak to the situation. If we do not know that what we want to pray for is in God's will, then ask him first —that is part of prayer. If we are still not sure, then we confess it and say nothing until we are sure —or pray in tongues. This can bring revelation.

If you think that God gives you sickness, then why go to the doctor? Surely would that in itself not then be sin? —to go against what you think is God's will for you! We must be sure that we know the authority that we have in the name of our Lord Jesus Christ. (See module 3.)

I asked a Christian doctor of medicine whether he considered it was God's will to heal, and he felt uncertain. I then asked him how he could therefore stay in practice if what he was doing in trying to make people well was against God's will!

Ask if people know that they are
—born again Christians;
—and under the anointing, i.e. baptised in the Spirit;
—and how they know this.

With all that girded around our loins, we can start to think about prayer.

2. *Put the heart diagram on the overhead projector and ask,* 'What do you think is meant by the following verses:

> *Search me, O God, and know my heart;*
> *test me and know my anxious thoughts.*
>
> (Psalm 139:23)

Petition
Create in me a pure heart... (Psalm.51:10).

Resolution
But in your hearts set apart Christ as Lord (1Peter.3:15).

Ask: Have you any doubt? Have you any fear? —fear of anything. Doubt and fear mean that we do not trust God in these areas of our lives.

Check out people's fears: water; heights; flying; poverty; spiders; men —and so on. Ask the class to tell about and discuss theirs. Use case studies to highlight fears and the healing of them.

In Psalm 139:23 (above)we read *test me and know my anxious thoughts*. How many of us can stand before we pray and ensure that we have no anxious thoughts? How often Jesus tells us not be anxious. Just do not do it! He does not even suggest that we ask Father to take it away. It is something we have to do for ourselves because, as he says, *Who of you by worrying can add a single hour to his life?* (Luke 12:25) and, as Paul writes, *Do not be anxious about anything, but in everything, by prayer and petition, with thanksgiving, present your requests to God* (Philippians 4:6). I could quote verse after verse saying virtually the same thing. Before you petition, stop being anxious. Fear and anxiety reveal the huge areas within our souls where we do not trust God. If we really, fully trusted that God would take care of everything and make it work for our benefit, then we would never again succumb to even the slightest twinge of anxiety. We get some clue of how to do this in the petition in Psalm 51:10 (see above); and the resolution: *But in your hearts set apart Christ as Lord. Always be prepared to give an answer to everyone who asks you to give the reason for the hope that you have. But do this with gentleness and respect* (1 Peter 3:15).

Mercifully, we have a Father who is full of grace and mercy, and a Lord Jesus who was even willing to die for us, to help us and do for us what we could never do in our own strength. This could be a very good time to ask Father to show you those things that you fear, and to help you get those fears out of your life for good. We have seen people healed of all kinds of fears, including: water, heights, men, flying, poverty, spiders and fire. We have seen release from agoraphobia, claustrophobia, and compulsive addictions —such as going round time and time again, to making sure the doors are locked or that the fire is out, and so on.

When we respond to what God requires of us, then we can appropriate what he desires for us. We need to understand the foundational principles, centring on the two areas forgiveness and acceptance, which are introduced here, and then we shall look at some practical examples.

3. *Ask what they understand of these fundamental principles:*

Forgiveness:
Of our sins
Of others
Of ourselves by God

Acceptance:
Of God as he really is
Of ourselves by ourselves
Of others

(When teaching this you may want to use case studies or examples from your own first hand experience)

Forgiveness

(i) As we know, our own sins need to be forgiven by God. This forgiveness is so freely available to all who come to the cross in repentance, with faith in the saving blood of Jesus.

(ii) We must forgive everyone else who has ever sinned against us or hurt or harmed us. This is an unconditional requirement.

(iii) We need to appropriate personally, inwardly, the reality, the truth of what Christ has done for us in his finished work on the cross. Sometimes this is expressed as 'forgiving ourselves', but in truth forgiveness could only have been won for us by Jesus, and we know forgiveness when we bring sin to the foot of the cross. What needs to happen is to really accept at the deepest level of our being that we are truly forgiven people, so eliminating false shame and false guilt. We need to come to a place of assurance that the forgiveness described in (1) above is done, it is real, it is finished and complete, not retaining in our heart any residual guilt in relation to what has been forgiven by God. We are to accept the release, which has been won for us, to truly enjoy the liberty that is God's gift for us.

(iv) We need to be released from any way in which we have blamed God for the bad things that have happened and that others have done to us. We may have asked why he did not stop the bad things happening. But we need to know that those bad things and bad actions did not come from God. They came from the disobedience of mankind, others' wrong choices, or from the enemy of God. God himself never hurts or harms us; he loves us with a perfect love. Sometimes what we have to do is expressed as 'forgiving God', but of course God does not need forgiving for anything. He is perfect, absolutely just, holy and merciful. We need to change our mind if our thinking has been wrong in this area; we need to be set free from the results of the blame we have wrongly ascribed to God; false declarations may need to be revoked, and countered with positive affirmations of trust in him who is perfectly good and loving towards us, and always has been, even when we were totally unaware of his love and felt very trapped and hurt.

Acceptance

It follows from the points above that acceptance must operate in our lives in these ways:

(i) We must accept God as he really is. (See [4] above.) Our minds are to be renewed as we study his word under the guidance of the Holy Spirit. Supremely, we begin to learn about the true character of God not from our own bad past experiences, which reveal man's sinful ways and this disobedient world, but rather from the truth the Father has revealed about his nature, in the person of Jesus Christ.

(ii) We must come to a real assurance that we are accepted by God. We may think ourselves unacceptable. If we had still been living in our sins, we would have been. But the Holy Spirit has led us to the point where we repented. God loved us so much that he has accepted us, and he is changing us, and he will go on changing us. Because we are forgiven sinners, we are acceptable to him; and not merely acceptable, but truly, lovingly, fully accepted as adopted precious children, members of his family. The hard thing is to change our minds and get used to thinking like this all the time! Compassionate ministry that constantly recalls us to the word of God on this point, and sometimes the deep work of the Holy Spirit, may be needed, to help us make this transition.

(iii) Flowing from this, we need to accept ourselves. Many are plagued and tormented by self-hatred, low self-image, low self-esteem, a sense of worthlessness. We need self-acceptance based on the sure foundation stated above.

(iv) We need to accept others. It is not enough just to have forgiven others. Our attitude to them must be like that of Christ Jesus. This can entail huge changes in all sorts of areas of our thinking, speaking and behaving. Acceptance does not mean approbation of all that others do; it does not mean agreeing with all they say. We are to be discerning and wise in our interactions with others. It does mean letting all our relationships be infused with godly, compassionate motivation. It does mean seeing and treating everyone else as having been created by God and loved by him, and sensing how he longs for them to come to know him as you have begun to know him.

Let us look a little more closely at what flows from some of those fundamental principles.

4. Look at what is laid up in our hearts and overflows

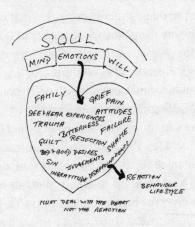

Examine all that might be included. With the help of the Holy

Spirit we need to be able to look at this in the light of Mark 11:24ff. *"Therefore I tell you, whatever you ask for in prayer, believe that you have received it, and it will be yours. And when you stand praying, if you hold anything against anyone, forgive him, so that your Father in heaven may forgive you your sins. But if you do not forgive, neither will your Father who is in heaven forgive your sins."* **Give the class a time to consider the implications of this for themselves and to ask God to highlight within them any instances, which need to be dealt with.** We need to look at what is laid up in our hearts and overflows out to others. The acts of the sinful nature are obvious: sexual immorality, impurity and debauchery; idolatry and witchcraft; hatred, discord, jealousy, fits of rage, selfish ambition, dissensions, factions and envy; drunkenness, orgies, and the like. I warn you, as I did before, that those who live like this will not inherit the kingdom of God. (Galatians 5:19ff). That is how Paul describes what human beings are naturally like inside, and when we add this to all the hurt, abuse, resentment, loneliness, and so many other experiences that may have been ours along the way, it makes us very careful how we present ourselves to the world. So much of the anger, the hurt, the rejection, the loneliness and everything else that is there inside us, often well hidden and camouflaged, will have come through situations and issues involving others.

We need to examine all that forgiveness and unforgiveness means. This includes the matter of the release from vows, particularly in relation to the breakdown of marriage. (See chapter 8 of The Anointing to Heal) Such an important part of this release involves being able to forgive the other partner. When we do so we need to be aware of all that forgiveness entails. Take, for instance, a man leaving his wife for another woman after maybe twenty-five years of marriage. They have grown-up children. To the jilted partner what has happened often seems worse than a bereavement. It was a matter of will on her husband's part to leave. This is total rejection of her and all they have had together. It trivialises the past, the early years of courtship, all the words of love he has said to her, the joy of the birth of their children, the wonderment years as the children grew up, and the exchanging of gifts. So many memories have been trampled underfoot and sullied. The list is endless and the hurt is deep. Then there are all the practicalities of the present: dealing with lawyers, courts, settlements, money, where and how to live, what to live for. Again, the list can be endless. Then there is the matter of the future. But what future? What about all the things that they planned to do together when the children left home, when they retired; the joy of planning together for their daughter's wedding and watching him lead their daughter down the aisle. So many more dreams now trampled underfoot and sullied. There is so much to be forgiven. When I was thinking about all that can be involved in forgiveness amid such devastation, I had the picture of the old-fashioned cartoon character of a burglar: a burly fellow, complete with striped jersey, mask over his eyes and a large sack over his shoulder, labelled 'swag'. The caption to the picture was: 'Stolen from me'. That expresses the feeling perfectly. It can feel as though someone has broken into all that we held dear and ransacked the whole place; we feel vandalised, and we feel empty inside, bereft of all that was meaningful.

So forgiveness is to be able to acknowledge all of this, recognise its deep importance and then let it go — completely. Again, do remember in this sort of practical context that forgiveness does not mean condoning or agreeing with the actions of any who hurt or abused us. Forgiveness is not releasing them from their own responsibility before God for their actions; they will still have to work those things out with Father themselves, and seek forgiveness for their own sin against God's law. What we are forgiving when we forgive them is what we can forgive: namely the harm done to us. To do this has the effect of releasing oneself.

The other option, unforgiveness, is allowing the abuser to have control over your life. It is like locking oneself up in solitary confinement in a high security prison cell and handing them the key. Forgiveness enables us to take the key back, and with it control over our own future. Unforgiveness can take some strange twists and turns but keeps us from wholeness and joy. We saw this on another of our overseas visits. But first, a cautionary note:

A word of warning

It is extremely important to be aware that if there is talk of forgiving someone who is now deceased, this must not entail speaking to – or attempting to communicate with – the one who has died. That is absolutely forbidden in the word of God. What is meant by such an expression, in any case where the person concerned has died, is by an act of will, a personal decision, doing away in our own hearts with any resentment, bitterness or sense of a debt to be paid, revoking any negative words and confessions we have made about the person, and replacing those with beliefs, declarations, attitudes that are in line with God's word rather than our own often very hurt and damaged feelings. So if we speak of 'forgiving' a dead person we are absolutely not to have some 'transaction' or 'communication' that involves them: we leave dealing with them to God alone, as has already been explained; we are to address what is going on in us, and we need to release ourselves from an ungodly heart attitude. To many this seems an impossible request. How can they forgive someone who has hurt, abused, slandered, them in the past or is continuing to do so? The prayer in 2 Thessalonians is that the Lord may direct your heart into the love of God, and in Jude 21 it is to keep ourselves in the love of God. So when we meet a situation where we realise that we really dislike someone or even hate someone, then we need to start reaching up to God, reaching up into the love of God. God loves them even when we cannot. Then we find a place in God's love where we can join him. I am not suggesting hypocrisy, where we simply say that we love or forgive somebody when we cannot truly mean it, hoping it will be enough. We reach into the place in our relationship with God which is sometimes expressed in liturgy as, 'by him, with him, in him and through him in the unity of the Holy Spirit'. This, then, is not just our love, this is God's love for us, ours for him, and in unity through him to them. Then, as we lift them up in God's love in our relationship with him, we pray blessings on them in the name of the Lord. We do this and go on doing this, and reaching out in God's love, until we get to the place where there is no reaction but love when we hear or think of their name or even meet them.

Hate can destroy our lives, bitterness can cripple us, dry up our whole lives so we become sickly and despondent. It eats away like a cancer and we feed it with our bitter thoughts so that whoever we hate begins to control our day, the way we think and act, so that we think of little else. We certainly are not then in any place to intercede for others. So we need to turn to God and ask his forgiveness as we lift them up to God's love. Refuse to think in hate – uproot it – wait anxiously for the mercy of our Lord Jesus Christ (Jude 21) – yield to the Spirit and bring the situation to the cross. Then we can love them truly. Not in our love but in the love of God. In natural love there is always a condition; his love is unconditional. The blood of Jesus protects us from the devil but the love of Jesus protects us from each other.

We went to The Hague: 'Honour your father and your mother'

Dorothy and I went to a European Convention of the FGBMFI. There came a time for ministry in the main convention hall itself and a man came over to me who was both very tall and quite large of girth. He said to me that he was born again and baptised in the Spirit but he did not know the fullness of joy. I laid my hand on his chest. Even if I had wanted to, I could not have laid my hand on his head, as he was much too tall. I prayed to Father for enlightenment. I had to say to the man that he had to give his father the place of honour in his heart, as we are instructed to in the commandments. The man started to cry. "How can I do that?" he said. "I am Jewish, I am French, and my father was a collaborator in the war. How can I honour my father?"

I replied with something along the following lines: Because God says we need to honour our father and our mother, it is not optional. It is a commandment, therefore it must be possible. It does not mean that you condone or forget what your father did, you just honour him in your own heart. Without him you would not be you. God honoured your father with the precious gift that is you. Perhaps he did not know how to properly cherish that gift. But the Frenchman could still not do it. I then asked him whether he was he willing to be made willing. He agreed to this and so, rather along the lines of 'Lord, I believe —help my unbelief', he prayed, "Lord I do not know how to honour my father, but I am willing to be made willing." There was a pause as I stood there with my hand on his chest. Then I felt rather than heard a rumbling starting in his tummy. This rumble developed more strongly and it coursed upwards through his large frame, finally erupting from his mouth in the loudest guffaw I have heard. He laughed and he laughed, as he now knew that fullness of joy!

Forgiving our son

Dorothy was away one Saturday and I was at home on my own. She had been given a pulpit from a decommissioned Methodist church, so I thought I would please her by re-erecting it in our garden room. Engaged in this, I was kneeling down when my back seized up. I was in excruciating pain. Only someone who has suffered on occasions with such a back problem will really understand how I felt. It was impossible for me to straighten up. It was totally impossible for me to even try to stand. I thought to myself that if I could crawl to the bathroom and lie in a hot tub for some time then it could possibly ease off. One big problem was that the bathroom was two floors above me. This meant that I had to mount two flights of stairs. I crawled to the bottom of the first flight. Then I felt God reminding me of the anger still within me following a strong altercation at work on the previous day with my eldest son. Father showed me that I was still retaining strong resentment towards my son, and that I must forgive him and let the anger and resentment go. I readily prayed and asked Father's forgiveness, releasing complete forgiveness. Immediately, the crippling pain was lifted and I was able to complete the building of the pulpit.

Forgiving work colleagues

Dorothy and I went to speak at a meeting in a city some distance away. A man came forward for ministry. He said that he worked in an office but now his right arm had tightened up in pain so he had difficulty in writing. I prayed to Father and was then able to say to the man that he had to forgive. The man thought for a while and could not think of anyone against whom he held any resentment. So I asked the Holy Spirit to lead us further. I was then able to tell the man that he needed to forgive his colleague at work. "Well," the man blustered, "it is all his fault. He sits straight opposite me at work. He says he is a Christian and yet he sits and smokes and blows smoke straight into my face." After this tirade subsided he was willing to pray a prayer of repentance and forgiveness. We did not have to speak to his arm: it was healed as he forgave!

Some other kinds of forgiveness we may need to release in our hearts are described elsewhere, including forgiveness of churches and those in authority. The ways in which we will need to release are manifold, and no list can be exhaustive. The important thing is always to be ready to forgive. 'Seventy times seven' means always and everywhere. Forgiveness must be a way of life, because God has forgiven us and he requires us to forgive others freely, willingly, joyfully and instantly. He will give anyone grace to do it if they are willing.

5. Is anyone carrying any guilt?

What we must remember is, *Therefore, there is now no condemnation for those who are in Christ Jesus...* (Romans 8:1). Why? *...because through Christ Jesus the law of the Spirit of life set me free from the law of sin and death* (Romans 8:2). *Dear friends, if our hearts do not condemn us, we have confidence before God and receive from him anything we ask, because we obey his commands and do what pleases him* (1 John 3:21f).

We need to examine ourselves and ask whether we have left any opening for Satan or sickness to come in. Remember that Satan is the accuser. He is going to lie, steal, cheat, and do anything he can to destroy all that should be ours in Christ Jesus. We should not carry guilt, shame or condemnation.

We must be sure to have stored up in our hearts these precious truths. I explained how I nearly put self condemnation on myself when accused by a colleague —I called myself a Christian and was going to carry guilt for terminating the employment of a manager. I have also told the story of the young mother who was in deep depression carrying guilt over the death of her daughter.

6. No self-justification

We also need to be clear that we are not maintaining self-justification. So many of us try to cover our own sins by blaming someone else, or maybe the situation in which we find ourselves. Here are a few examples:

'I would go to church on Sunday mornings but all the family lie in bed late, so they prevent me from doing so.'
'If only my husband would become a Christian, then I could do Bible study.'
'If only my wife were more affectionate towards me I would not need to have an affair with the girl in the office.'
'If only my husband did not drink so much, I could cut down as well.'
'If only everyone was nicer to me I would not need to tell lies.'
'If only I got paid more I would not have to cheat on the benefits.'

Just ask the Lord what your own 'if onlys' are. Then deal with the matter by repenting of the heart attitude, revoking the 'if only', and making positive faith-filled confessions instead.

7. What do we mean by negative confession?

In Numbers 14 the land is full of giants. How many times have you said or thought to yourself things like these—
'Oh, I could never do that.'
'I am not brainy enough for that.'
'I could never stand up in front of all those people.'
'I cannot even butter bread or boil and egg.'

'I could never walk in a room on my own.' —and so on.

These are negative confessions, and when we say such things we are really cursing ourselves. Whereas when we are born again the fact is— *I can do everything through him who gives me strength* (Philippians 4:13). We need to ask God to release us from such curses, with the blood of Jesus as full payment, because Jesus was made a curse for us on the cross so that man need no longer live under a curse.

Although shyness is often looked upon as being an acceptable or even attractive trait, is it in fact not a sin? Rather than being true humility, is it not more an attitude of pride? A shy person may, for example, be afraid to enter a room because they feel that everyone will be looking at them. They need to repent of their expectation to be the centre of attention —then ask Father to forgive them for allowing their wills to be dominated by the fear of man or woman. Once they have the absolution, they should tell the spirit of domination to leave them because it has no authority any longer to hold them in bondage.

8. *Ask whether anyone has had any occult or secret society involvement*
Talk about the need for release from any occult involvement, and what that might be. Also: secret societies (masons, etc.);
Cleansing the house or self of any artefacts. Check out whether you or any of the family you know about has had any occult or secret society involvement. If so, go before the Lord, cut off and renounce any such links, and revoke any ungodly vows, pleading the blood of Jesus. Then ask for a fresh infilling of the Holy Spirit. Have a check around the house to see if there are any artefacts, books, things that should not be there because of their connections, and, if possible, burn

them, but in any event permanently destroy them. (Needless to say, you should not pass them on to anyone else)

In Houston

On a Saturday morning I had done a session on blessings and curses, and mentioned secret societies. Annie had prophesied about some freemasonry artefacts that some people had, including a box. That afternoon a brother and sister came forward to testify that they had gone home at lunchtime and destroyed a box which had held masonic regalia from a relative. Also, they were getting rid of a large portrait of a dead relative on which his masonic ring was prominently displayed.

At home

Literally in our own home, on the hearth, were two carved fertility figures which I had purchased when we lived in West Africa. Dorothy never liked these, and when we turned to Christ she was never happy with them in the house. As we learned more about the dangers of the occult, she became the more eager to get them out of the house, but as they were mine she could not touch them until I agreed. When I said that she could dispose of them, she took them into the garden and tried to chop them into pieces, but nearly wrenched her arm and could make no impression on them. Then she recalled that the Lord had told her to burn them, but, try as she might, she was not able to set light to them. The Lord showed her that they were under the power of Satan, so she prayed to break Satan's power. The figures flared up like tinder and were destroyed.

9. Do you feel and think that others are more worthy or needy, or have a better case to be healed than you?

FACT — God is impartial.

For God does not show favoritism (Romans 2:11).

Then Peter began to speak: "I now realize how true it is that God does not show favoritism" (Acts 10:34).

...who wants all men to be saved and to come to a knowledge of the truth (1 Timothy 2:4).

"For God so loved the world that he gave his one and only Son, that whoever believes in him shall not perish but have eternal life" (John 3:16).

And we have seen and testify that the Father has sent his Son to be the Savior of the world (1 John 4:14).

Check out whether you feel that others are more worthy or more needy, or have a better case to be healed than you. So many really nice people are ready to pray for others but feel that what they have is too trivial, compared with the needs of others, to bother God. Then there are cases where some people are annoyed that others seem to get healed when they do not, and they think God must not love them as much as he does the others. That serious error causes much unnecessary grief. Remember that God is impartial. (See the passages cited above.)

When you pray, be assured God loves us equally; he wants you to receive the healing that Jesus won for you on the cross as much as he does everyone else. He wants all to be saved and to come to a knowledge of the truth. (See 1 Timothy 2:4.) And remember that he so loved the world that he gave his one and only Son, that whoever believes in him shall not perish but have eternal life. (See John 3:16). Believe that it is God's nature and will to heal.

8

LISTENING TO GOD

Ask for, and write up on board, questions people have about this issue, and see if they have all been addressed by the end of the session.

Session 1

A. How can I know that God speaks?
Everything we need comes from God, Our spiritual life, the ways in which to live it, how to understand and recognise the things of God, all come through the Holy Spirit —everything! From the beginning we can see in Scripture that the way in which this was communicated was a very personal one. God set up the system. He created the environment for his most beloved creation to live in —that is you and me. Adam was the first one, the representative person of man, and God told him all about it. If Adam had any queries there was this personal relationship. God himself came down daily to walk in the garden and talk things over with Adam, to have fellowship with him. There is some way in which God puts himself across our path every

115

day, so that we can sort things out with him. It was not just an opportunity for Adam to report on what he had been doing but it was a time for them to get together and enjoy a personal relationship, an easy, direct communication with each other.

Later, after the Fall, when Adam's spirit was separated from God's Spirit, that was the death. God then spoke to people through intermediaries. When he wanted to communicate his law, it was to Moses that he gave the commandments, written on stones, to guide the people. Moses was the intermediary. The whole purpose of the law was to show man that he could not live separated from God. It was not about saying that if you keep these commandments you will be fine, because in fact they are impossible to keep. God was setting up a structure in which people could live, but there was always going to be an awareness of lack, an awareness of failure on my part, and that is quite crucial. It is the emptiness of being separated from God that is always going to be pressed on, in our lives, especially after we are born again. We must be aware that, even though we want to know everything about him, especially when we are new Christians, we do not —and we do not need to. Over time, line by line, precept upon precept, as it says in the Bible, he will reveal more and more of himself to us. The main points are that he does know everything and that we have access to him.

B. How can I be sure he wants to speak to me?

Later again, Jesus became the intermediary, and began to reinstate the personal way of communication. Until then, communication with God had been mainly through the prophets. People would go to the prophets and ask what God was saying. People do that today —and we really should not, those are Old Testament ways. We need to go to God for ourselves. (See Module 4 on the gifts of the Spirit.) We are in the Adam position again, where he is going to come to have fellowship with us. If we wait on him, then he comes to us. The first spiritual principle is that we love because he first loved us; we have because he has first given. We can give because we have first received. Everything centres on him; he is pivotal.

As was the custom for young rabbis, Jesus taught a band of disciples. Unlike the custom however, they did not apply to follow him, they were not rigorously tested on the Torah, they did not have to be word perfect in their answers. He chose them, he called them to him. Before Jesus' earthly ministry, in order to become a disciple you had to be able to *do* —whereas to become a disciple of Jesus we just have to *be*. We do not have to pass any tests of knowledge to become a Christian; we do not have to know anything, we just have to say yes and follow him. The disciples had to give up everything and follow him. Go to the Scriptures, and see how he called to them and they responded.

Jesus opened up a whole new way. He chose the disciples himself, after spending the night in solitude with Father, and all they had to do was to follow him and learn from him. After a while, when they had listened to him and watched him at work, he blessed them and sent them out to do precisely the same things in the same ways that he did. They followed the same methods, although 'methods' is not a good word, I tend to call them 'models'. 'Methods' sounds as if there is a rulebook of how to go and minister to people, but we should know that that is not the way it works. We have to listen because every situation is fresh. The Scripture says that he is new every morning and he is faithful. Every single day is different, no matter how it seems like the day before. Every situation and interaction in prayer with other people, which is what we are talking about, is the healing ministry of the Holy Spirit. We cannot go and be of service to anyone before we have first been served by him. It is that same principle that was mentioned before: we can only serve God because he has first served us. We need to know the Servant king before we can become servants. Jesus first sent the 12 and then 72, and they came back cock a hoop because they had met with acceptance from God and had briefly touched and been touched by him in power. Disciples are learners, and we must remember that we too are learners, and always will be. We will never know it all, but will always need to depend upon Father and look to see what he is saying to us.

It is exactly so for all disciples today. The way of Jesus, is the way of the Spirit. It is to the Holy Spirit we must each look for guidance. It is the Holy Spirit who reveals Jesus to us, and it is Jesus who takes us into the Father's presence. Father God then involves us in his works just like he did with Jesus. Through Jesus we were shown how to relate to God as our Father. With deepening communication, we also should begin to be able to speak to the Father as Jesus did. *Jesus gave them this answer: "I tell you the truth, the Son can do nothing by himself; he can do only what he sees his Father doing, because whatever the Father does the Son also does* (John 5:19).

The work that God asks us to do is to believe in Jesus. Then he can do things beyond our imagination according to the power he has put with us. (See Ephesians 3:20.)

Jesus modeled the life of an obedient son. When he was preparing to leave and go back to heaven, he pointed his followers to the coming of the Holy Spirit. *And I will ask the Father...* (John 14:16). It is absolutely vital that we ask Father. He loves to be asked, and it is a release mechanism for us when we ask: 'Please may I have...'; Please will you do...'; 'Please will you show me....' When we do this it begins to develop the habit of depending upon God, looking to him always as the first point of resource. This is particularly highlighted at times when we have a breakdown in communication with other people.

Jesus gives you: *...another Counsellor, to be with you forever, the Spirit of truth. The world cannot accept him, because it neither sees him nor knows him. But you know him, for he lives with you and will be in you.* We know from Scripture that it is the truth which sets us free. Sometimes, when he reveals the truth to us about ourselves, possibly with regard to how nasty we can be, it can feel quite horrid. But if we acknowledge it, and start working with him on it, we find that it was not to diminish us but to take us out from the brokenness and build us up. Never feel condemned by the Holy Spirit, but accept that he is showing us so that we can respond, repent by acknowledging the truth, and then, with his guidance, determine to turn away from what is wrong. We need to bind our minds to the mind of Christ, so that we start to think and act like him.

It was to be the Holy Spirit who would come to lead the church – lead us, because we are the church – into all truth, the truth which would set us free to be with God and be used in the works of God here on earth.

C. How can I listen to him?

So to listen to God is to be acquainted intimately with the Holy Spirit, for he knows the hearts of men. As the Holy Spirit begins to feed our spirit, our spirit begins to know our heart too. He is the one who brings us to the place of reconciliation with God, by revealing to us the truth of our need of God; and, having done this, he reveals that this way is through the life of Jesus. We should never think or dream of doing anything without the Holy Spirit to guide and empower us.

To listen to God as a child of his, we must all have gone through this process with the Holy Spirit, where he reveals our need of Jesus and our willingness to give up everything about our former lives in order to receive him: that is, climaxing with a new birth —being 'born again from on high' as Scripture describes it. This is birth into a new life in the Spirit, based on his purity, and everything in us, of experience or belief, must come under the authority of the Holy Spirit, so that we become ordered in the right way. Our human spirit is to be under the direction of the Holy Spirit, our souls and bodies under the direction of our spirit. The first question we need to ask of ourselves, in order to be sure of our position with God and his equipping to go out in his name and minister through the power of his Spirit is this:

D. Have I been born again of the Holy Spirit, into the life of Jesus? If the answer is yes, then we know we have a sure foundation (Jesus) for listening to God. We have become sons and heirs with him. Thus we can converse with God and we can be sure that we listen and hear him. Jesus said, *My sheep listen to my voice; I know them, and they follow me* (John 10:27). If the answer is no, then the opposite applies. We are not yet sheep. We cannot listen to Jesus and we do not follow him as our leader. In the same passage Jesus says, ...*but you do not believe because you are not my sheep* (John 10:26). So this point needs to be resolved by you with God before continuing. The second question is:

E. How can I be sure that God will speak to me?
Most people have a difficulty here. They can believe that God speaks to other people —but to themselves? They are not sure. All through Scripture there is evidence of the desire of God to speak to us. *Listen, listen to me, and eat what is good, and your soul will delight in the richest of fare* (Isaiah 55:2b). *Listen, my son, to your father's instruction and do not forsake your mother's teaching* (Proverbs 1:8). *Listen, my sons, to a father's instruction; pay attention and gain understanding. I give you sound learning, so do not forsake my teaching* (Proverbs 4:1f).

My son, pay attention to my wisdom, listen well to my words of insight (Proverbs 5:1) *Now then, my sons, listen to me; do not turn aside from what I say* (Proverbs 5:7).

God spoke to Adam, Abraham, Moses, Joshua and many others. He spoke to Jesus, Peter, Paul, and so on right down through he ages. He wants to speak to us; he wants to communicate with us. He knows just how to do so with each individual. He speaks through the Scriptures as the Holy Spirit quickens them to us. Probably if each of us reads the same passage from Scripture we will each have a slightly different view of what God is saying through it. But he also speaks outside of Scripture in a very personal and individual way to his children. Remember, God knows you in a way that no human can, so he can say things in a way, which is particularly relevant to you. These personal ways will not conflict with scriptural teaching, but they are so 'ordinary' to us that we often doubt them. Can God really be telling me where I have put my car keys? Or point me to a parking space when I have a real need for one? Give me words of encouragement and comfort which get right to the root of a situation? The answer is an emphatic YES! He does speak to us. *So they took away the stone. Then Jesus looked up and said, "Father, I thank you that you have heard me. I knew that you always hear me, but I said this for the benefit of the people standing here, that they may believe that you sent me"* (John 11:41). It was immediately after this that Jesus called on Lazarus to come out of the tomb. Now the relevant question here is this:

F. Have you found these words to be true in your experience?

This assurance is your tool bag into which he puts all the gifts you will need to minister in his name. Without this foundation and constant equipping, we will never minister with power, rather with timidity and tentativeness, not with the authority Jesus has conferred on his followers who believe him. So here we really do have a choice to make. Do I believe he hears me and I hear him? When you pray, have you seen the signs accompanying you, the signs Jesus said would be there for those who believed in him? (Refer to Mark16:17.)

We really do need to learn to move so assuredly in all of this: God's will; God's knowledge of us; his purposes. We need to trust the leading of the Holy Spirit —and feel secure in him. This equipping can only come about as a result of our intimate relationship with him. You can only listen to him if you are with him. It cannot be emphasised too often that we need to spend time with God. The most important thing is for our heart. Jesus taught that if we love him we will keep his commandments.

We need to be aware of self and flesh issues where we need to confess and repent, and be ready to exercise our wills to obey the will of God. They have to be exercised towards him because sometimes our wills are set against him.

The Holy Spirit will instruct us in what we need to know to resist Satan and the demonic forces. We do not have to go overboard and get so fixated on Satan that we pay too much attention to the enemy, rather than fixing our eyes on Jesus.

As to the ways of the world and the negative pressures that arise from them, recognise that because you a Christian, a member of the body of Christ, you are in the kingdom, but 'the world' is opposed to the kingdom, which is God's perfect rule. As we minister to others the good things of the kingdom, in the power of the Holy Spirit, we become potential points of wholeness and healing for others.

Session 2
Get the delegates to work individually and respond to the following questions on a handout. (Allow 20 minutes.)

A. Personal inventory

How do I hear him most easily?

When do I hear him?

Where do I hear him?

What is the most recent thing he has said?

How did I respond?

Do signs accompany me when I pray?

Which signs have I seen after I have prayed?

What is in my mind/heart as I pray for others?......

Confidence? In what or whom?

Timidity? —For what reason and what do I do about it?

Anxiety? —For what reason and what do I do about it?

B. Praying for others

Questions to consider:

Am I secure in knowing God speaks to me? Am I working under authority in praying for others? (Or willing to be so.) Am I willing to be questioned/held accountable?

This is most important if I am seeking him on behalf of others. If this is all new to you, or if you feel uncertain what should you do? In the context of the Healing Centre, tell one of the directors and arrange with them to work alongside someone else with a view to gaining experience. This will involve feedback from your partner: checking out what you say; learning how to offer the words or pictures you believe you are receiving with the person being prayed for; being careful to give only what you have been given, and not to interpret the content; reporting to the directors as part of your accountability structure. If you are not working at the Centre, then ask for this sort of opportunity and oversight from your church leader. Following Jesus' pattern of training, it is better to work with a partner wherever possible. Always work under authority. You need to be accountable and answer for the words you are speaking into someone else's life, and they need the security of having a place they can go to question or complain, or for further explanation.

Session 3

Who is called to heal the sick?

Each one of us has been called into service. There are no exceptions. It is not optional, or only a call given to special believers, or mature believers, or so-called important believers. *He said to them, "Go into all the world and preach the good news to all creation. And these signs will accompany those who believe: In my name they will drive out demons; they will speak in new tongues; they will pick up snakes with their hands; and when they drink deadly poison, it will not hurt them at all; they will place their hands on sick people, and they will get well"* (Mark 16:15ff).

A. Knowing how to pray when ministering

The best preparation is personal intimacy with God through times spent with him, through Scripture reading and growing in familiarity with the ways of God and the life of Jesus. The Holy Spirit will teach us, give us revelation, and release his gifts into our lives during these times of intimacy. We also grow as we meet with and are ministered to by, other Christians. When we then come to pray with others we will have a rising confidence in knowing we hear God and in applying what he shows us or tells us to do..

B. How sure am I of what I am hearing and its source (God, the devil or self?)

Four crucial elements:

Do a question time and write up on board the answers, then make sure that at least the following 4 basics are covered.

This is where your personal relationship with God is crucial.

(1) The habit of asking the Holy Spirit to search your heart is essential.

(2) Regular reading of Scripture is crucial, as this is where we find the will of God written down for us to find.

(3) Study (as well as reading) of God's word is crucial so that you can be more deeply instructed.

(4) Obedience to the will of God as you find it and understand is crucial.

Read Psalm 139. Consider God's perfect knowledge of man, and man's response to that. We need to be sure and aware of God's constant presence, but also sure and aware of our own evil, and aware of demonic presence or activity when it occurs. We need to recognise what is happening when we are praying, able to trust and feel secure in the leading of the Holy Spirit. This comes about as a result of relationship with God, and this happens as we apply our time and attention. It will not come about because we listen to the odd sermon, or toss up the odd prayer. Like every relationship it deepens and grows with time, attention, understanding, giving and receiving. And this is how it must be if we are to be used as effective channels by God.

(a) Being perfected; searching your heart; examining your conscience; making your confession —are all terms to describe a cleansing process which makes and keeps us sensitive to God.

(b) Meditation and contemplation are ways of being nourished by him.

(c) Obedience to God's ways, keeping his laws is essential. Loving God is really what it is all about. *"If you love me you will keep my commandments"* said Jesus. So obedience is a sign of active love towards God. Proverbs 4 says, *'My son, keep my words before your eyes... they are life to you when you find them and healing to your whole body'* (paraphrased).

Being instructed in these ways, makes one aware of the love of God and the ways of enmity with God namely:

(i) Self or 'flesh issues where we need to confess and repent. Exercising our wills to the will and ways of God;

(ii) The nature and ways of Satan and demonic forces and structures;

(iii) The ways of the world and the negative pressures that arise from them.

Conclusion

Nobody is perfect when they start to pray for others, and even after years of doing it, responding to the Holy Spirit, still no-one is perfect. But we are being perfected, we are being changed by God from one degree of his glory or presence to another degree. This is a continuous process, which will be completed only when we get to heaven. So the high standard is not something which should put us off, rather it should encourage us beckon us forward. We cannot perfect ourselves, only God can do that, and he will if we start to respond to him.

How do I listen to the person but also to the Holy Spirit? Basically, by accepting what the person says as your starting point, but immediately submitting it to the Holy Spirit for direction as to how to proceed, then waiting until you have that direction.

Looking at any aspect of the healing ministry almost always gets us in touch with areas of ignorance or lack. This is the way the Holy Spirit leads us on, to seek after truth, to be taught by him, to implement what he is teaching us.

Most meals are taken in bite sized pieces until they are finished. We eat at regular intervals, rather than in one fell swoop. We also like to vary our intake, to have variety, and food in season is one of the pleasures of eating. It is so in the Spirit, too. 'Taste and see that the Lord is good.' 'He brought me to his banqueting table.' 'He sets a table for me before my enemies.'

There is a time for everything, we are told in Ecclesiastes, and so it is with our learning and growth patterns in the Spirit. We need to do what we can, not worry about what we cannot. Starting from where we are is all we can do, and in God's eyes it is enough.

As it is his plan and his power, his goals and his ways, all we have to do is tuck in there with him, following and obeying as he gives us direction and understanding.

9

HEALING THROUGH WORSHIP

Introduction

At virtually every healing service, music is an integral part. So we have to ask ourselves why this is the case. What is so important about worship music that few services, healing or otherwise, seem to be held without it? What part does it play —for the minister and for the one receiving ministry?

1. Worship: focussing on God, not on self

Then Jesus said to his disciples, "If anyone would come after me, he must deny himself and take up his cross and follow me. For whoever wants to save his life will lose it, but whoever loses his life for me will find it" (Matthew 16:24f).

Therefore, I urge you, brothers, in view of God's mercy, to offer your bodies as living sacrifices, holy and pleasing to God—this is your spiritual act of worship. Do not conform any longer to the pattern of this world, but be transformed by the renewing of your mind. Then you will be able to test and approve what God's will is—his good, pleasing and perfect will (Romans 12:1f).

I mention this at the outset because it is absolutely prime in everything we are going to consider. Worship is what we are about. Worship is what God put us here for and it is integral to our very nature. The big sin that started off all the problems in the first place was that Satan wanted to be worshipped. That is a big all time no-no. So, as we start a module on worship in healing, let us set out very clearly for ourselves that none of what we do is for us. None of it is for the people who come for ministry. It is all, 100%, completely, for God. If we notice any sense of wanting to be noticed ourselves – for how hard we have worked, or how many people got really blessed, or anything else in that line that you can think of – then we need to confess to God that we are sorry that we have moved our focus away from him for a little and then get focussed right back in on God. We worship him and we look for no commendation in so doing: this is all about giving all our focus and all our attention to God. And that is worship

2. Temple worship

There are many 'types' in the OT. Types are those things which were true for the day and also foreshadowed things that would come later in the Christian era as well, in a different form but with the same flavour or underlying principles. For example, the near sacrifice of Isaac by Abraham was both an actual event and also a type, foreshadowing what God the Father was doing in sending God the Son. The temple is another type. It was a style of worship for the Jews in the days of King Solomon right down to the days of Jesus, and it also foreshadowed Christian worship. So, a quick look at temple worship.

The glory of the temple

King David wanted to build God a permanent house, but God still lived in his tent. God said to David that Solomon would build the temple. (See 1Chron 22:8.) So David decided to lay up the treasure for it.

(a) 1 Chron 22:5 David wanted the whole thing to be 'forget the budget' big!

(b) v 14 silver & gold = £65 billion plus immeasurable other stuff. David gave c. £1.6 billion from his own bank account (See 1Chron 29:1–4.)

The music of the temple

Prophetic

(a) Prophets as ordered by the king (1Chron 25:1–2)

(b) Prophets who give thanks to God (v 3)

(c) Prophets (seers) who exalt God's 'horn' (v 5)

Ordered

(a) 4000 worship singers (1Chron 23:5)

(b) 288 skilled musicians (vv 7–8)

(c) Divided into a rota (v 8); 24 rota slots (cf. 24:3, 19)

(d) Specific worship roles were assigned each person (1 Chron 15:16–21)

Points to note

The temple was lavish. God wanted it to be an awesome place that people came into to worship. If you do a study on the tabernacle, you will see that it too was a truly outstanding and awesome tent.

God expects praise & worship 24/7 from his congregations and puts worship leaders within the body to enable worship. There was always worship in the temple, whether there was a service going on or not!

There is nothing slapdash about the way God wants worship conducted. He had 24 hour a day, professional musicians conducting worship in his temple. (See 1Chron 9:33; 16:41.) So why should we be any different?

It was the Levites, not the priests, who offered worship. That is, the laity.

Now go to Matt 27:51 where the veil is torn asunder and so all God's people can now come into intimate close communion with God.

3. Worship in heaven

(a) Isaiah 6:1–4
- **Smoke-filled, like the incense filled temple**
- **God sitting enthroned like in the Holy of Holies**
- **Continual praises being sung**

(b) Revelation 4:7–11
- **24/7 worship**
- **God's praises continually sung**
- **God alone is the object of focus**

(c) Revelation 7:9–17
- **worship from all tribes and nations**
- **Jesus, the Lamb, is at the centre of the praise**
- **it's very loud**

(d) Revelation 8:1–6
- **An unusual event – silence in heaven**
- **If he has to say there was silence for half an hour, does that mean that there had not been silence at all up to this point? If the 24/7 worship in the temple reflected the worship in heaven, then worship is 24/7 in heaven too**

(e) Revelation 11:15–19
- **ark of the covenant in the temple**
- **great earthquakes, thunderings and lightnings**
- **loud praise of God and the Lamb going on**

(f) Revelation 14:1–5
- **singing a new song - some just want the old classics but there's new stuff to be learned**
- **Jesus' voice is like the sound of many waters – it's very loud**

(g) Revelation 15:1–4
- **They sing the song of Moses – some just want the most recent but the classics are in heaven too**

(h) Revelation 19:1–10
- **Praise is testimony**
- **Behind testimony is the Holy Spirit**
- **Where the Holy Spirit is, there is power**

4. Praise or worship —both defined biblically

It may surprise you to know this, but praise and worship in the Bible are not the same thing. There are many words for praise in the OT, and we will look at some of them; there is one word only in each of the OT and NT for worship.

(a) **Praise words**

HALAL = to praise Yahweh = to praise God.

Has sense of boastful, excited, to enjoy. Cf. David dancing before the ark and his wife Michal taking offence at his cavorting.

YADAH

Ps 138:1 = public acknowledgement

Exciting throwing up of arms. Cf. 2 Chron 20
BARAK To bless
Ps 103:1-2 Bless the Lord O my soul
Sense of kneeling and bowing
ZAMAR
Music making to God = to touch the strings
Ps 150
SHABACH
Ps 117:1
To laud, speak well of; to address loudly, to shout, to glory
TOWDAH
Thanksgiving for past & future help
Therefore an act of faith
Praise now for salvation later
TEHILLAH
To sing, to laud
Singing halals
Ps 22:3 and 2 Chron 20:22
Unprepared singing = singing in the Spirit
RUAH
To shout in joy
Ps 95:1 and 100:1
QARA
Proclamation
Ps 116:17
NAGAD = to declare Ps 9:11b
BASAR = to proclaim
RUM = to extol

(b) **Worship words**

OT (Hebrew) word is *shachah*. This occurs 172 times, 2 of which mean to crouch (1 Sam 2:36) or to stoop (Prov 12:25). The other 170 mean to worship, to bow down, to do obeisance, to reverence, to fall down (before).

NT (Greek) word is *proskuneo*. All 60 occasions are translated as worship.

Both of these have the idea of deferring to one greater than yourself. They incorporate the action of bowing down before in homage. To worship, then, is to give the place of honour and esteem to another, in both words and action. There is no place for self —self-consciousness, self-centredness, self-acknowledgement etc. All our attention and thoughts and feelings are focussed on acknowledging the one who is the object of our worship.

5. Conclusions so far

(a) **Worship is what we are about**

(b) **God has ordained worship as an integral and important part of our life**

(c) **Worship goes on in heaven**

(d) **Worship is often (more often than not) noisy**

(e) **Worship involves the whole person**

(f) **Praising God can lead to intense worship, e.g. Rev 19**

(g) **Worship is to be lavish**

(h) **Worship should be wholehearted and fully entered into**

Worship has a physical effect – thunderings in heaven: physical well being brought on through exercise

6. Effects of praise and worship

(a) Josh 6:1–21
- **Praise and the presence of God (signified by the ark) was God's battle plan**
- **When they shouted and blew, the walls came down**
- **Then the soldiers went out to battle**

(b) 1 Chron 20
- **They fasted – a form of worship**
- **They praised – O God, our father of Abraham, etc**
- **There was a prophetic word, v 17**
- **v 18 – they worshiped again**
- **They went out to battle praising the beauty of holiness**
- **God beat the enemy.**

(c) Acts 2:42–47
- **Continued in fellowship and worship**
- **Signs and wonders followed on**

And they continued steadfastly in the apostles' doctrine and fellowship, in the breaking of bread, and in prayers. Then fear came upon every soul, and many wonders and signs were done through the apostles. Now all who believed were together, and had all things in common, and sold their possessions and goods, and divided them among all, as anyone had need. So continuing daily with one accord in the temple, and breaking bread from house to house, they ate their food with gladness and simplicity of heart, praising God and having favor with all the people. And the Lord added to the church daily those who were being saved.

(d) Acts 3:1–9
- **On the way to worship**
- **Signs and wonders – a healing**

(e) Acts 3:11–4:4
- **Went to worship**
- **This gave an opportunity to preach**
- **Some persecution – they were arrested**
- **But many were saved that day**

(f) Acts 4:23–31
- **Following their release, the believers got together for a praise party**
- **The presence of God was seen, as in the days of Solomon and in the readings about heaven**
- **They went about speaking the word boldly as a result**

(g) Acts 16:24–26
- **Paul and Silas having a praise party in prison**
- **This produces an earthquake which opens the doors; and also their chains fell off**
- **They then have an opportunity to preach**
- **The jailer and all his household are saved**

(h) 1 Sam 16:22–23
- **Anointed playing brings healing**

(i) Ex 17:8–13
Moses' hands up = a praise and worship position – victory
Moses' hands down = defeat

7. The power of agreement in praise and worship

(a)   *Yet you are enthroned as the Holy One;*
         you are the praise of Israel (Ps 22:3).

(b) "When praise and worship is loosed by a group, there is a tremendous amount of power generated. Ps 22:3 says that God inhabits the praises of his people. When we praise God together, God inhabits our praise. Because corporate praise involves the power of agreement, the power of coming into harmony, there is a tremendous spiritual energy generated." (Terry Law, *The Power of Praise and Worship*)

(c) See Acts 4:32–37:
Held all things in common
Power accompanied the apostles' preaching
None lacked

(d) See Acts 5:12–16.
They met in the temple
They were in one accord
Believers added daily
All that came were healed
Many signs and wonders were done among the people, including the sick in the street healed as Peter's shadow fell on them

(e) *"Again, I tell you that if two of you on earth agree about anything you ask for, it will be done for you by my Father in heaven. For where two or three come together in my name, there am I with them"* (Matthew 18:19f).

(f) See 2 Corinthians 10:4. *The weapons we fight with are not the weapons of the world. On the contrary, they have divine power to demolish strongholds.*

And one of those weapons is praise and worship

(g) **Praising is as important to us as eating and breathing**

(h) **Jesus prayed and then healed**
So they took away the stone. Then Jesus looked up and said, "Father, I thank you that you have heard me. I knew that you always hear me, but I said this for the benefit of the people standing here, that they may believe that you sent me." When he had said this, Jesus called in a loud voice, "Lazarus, come

out!" The dead man came out, his hands and feet wrapped with strips of linen, and a cloth around his face. Jesus said to them, "Take off the grave clothes and let him go" (John 11:41–44).

Question
Is there something going on in heaven between and praise happening and signs and wonders bringing victory in all facets of life? Yes!

8. Conclusions
- **God is present when we come together.**
- **Praise and worship brings us together in one accord.**
- **Setting our activity into praise and worship puts us in a place to receive.**
- **God will perform signs and wonders when we praise his name. We should expect the unexpected when we enter into praise and worship.**
- **The supernatural will become the norm if we dedicate ourselves to worship.**

9. Practical
A few songs from the hymnody of the group shold be chosen for half an hour's worship and three that I have successfully used in the past are: *He is the Lord*; *All hail the Lamb*; *I see the Lord*.

TRAINING WHEEL PRAYERS FOR SITUATIONS

These are what my friend Liberty Savard would call training wheel prayers. There is no defined way of praying. In time, and/or in order to cover particular or peculiar situations that you meet, you will undoubtedly, with the help of the Holy Spirit, evolve your own style of praying. In the meantime, practice with these will bring you into compliance with the will of Father God and the power and authority in Jesus' name. Remember Ephesians 3:20, *Now to him who is able to do immeasurably more than all we ask or imagine, according to his power that is at work within us*. As we pray in Jesus' name, his power at work within us can do more than we can imagine. According to Module 7 (Be Clear for Prayer), we start with our prayer to release unforgiveness within us.

Prayers

To forgive

Father God I want to totally forgive from the bottom of my heart all the people whoever did me any harm —or against whom I have resentment and bitterness. I especially name [............]. Please help me through your grace where I am still not healed and willing. In Jesus' name, I release them all. I forgive them totally from my heart.

Also, Father, I ask you to forgive me for the times I have blamed you.

Father, where I have been in self-condemnation and blamed myself, even after asking for and receivingyour forgiveness: I accept forgiveness of myself for everything for which you have already forgiven me. In Jesus' name, I receive your forgiveness for once and for all. I am free in Jesus name.

Release from occult

Father God, I repent utterly of any occult involvement which I have had in my life. (Name the situations, e.g. fortune telling; involvemment in secret societies; reading horoscopes, etc.) and any other which I cannot remember or have not recognised – make me aware of them and forgive me, cleanse me and set me free in Jesus' name..

Freedom from domination

To release from domination

Father God, you gave me the gift of free will and I claim, in the name of Jesus, that it is my wish and intention from now onwards to keep my freedom of will to make decisions. The only person I ever want to submit my will to is you Lord, and so I bind my will to your will, and my mind to the mind of Christ. I am sorry and I repent of every time when, even as a child, I have allowed my will to be dominated by others. I repent of it. Forgive me in the name of Jesus, and I ask you to set me free. I order and command every spirit of domination that is keeping me in submission to leave me so that I will be free. The only one to whom I will bind my will from this time forth will be you, Lord Jesus. I praise and bless your name.

Freedom from rejection

Release from strongholds and carnal defences

Father God, help me, through your grace and mercy and power to pull down, smash, crush and destroy all the strongholds I have built to guard my carnal desires. In particular [name them, e.g. withdrawal, anger, criticism, sarcasm, or any other.] I renounce them; I repent of them. Forgive me for ever using them. Thank you Lord Jesus, and as I use the keys of the kingdom to loose them from me and set myself free, I ask you to set me free from any power of the enemy which has had the authority to oppress me through them. Please replace them from heaven with grace, mercy, peace, soundness of mind, self-control, love, joy and all the other blessings you have made available for me. Thank you Jesus.

If the person is saying these prayers during a ministry session then you as the prayer minister might say: 'In the name of Jesus. As these strongholds are pulled down I stand against every spirit of darkness which has oppressed this person. I command it to go from them in Jesus name.'

The person being ministered to will now say:
Almighty God, I do not want to build any more strongholds and it is my desire to make you my sole defence – my fortress; the shield of my heart – so that nothing whatsoever can happen to me outside of your Divine Providence and your love. Thank you Jesus.

Hurt and rejection
Lord Jesus, You suffered rejection by your people on the cross. I ask you now to remove from their heart, mind and spirit all of the rejection, the anguish, the pain, they have ever experienced, even back to the time when they were conceived in the womb, and release them into the freedom, wholeness and joy of being themselves. Holy Spirit, as the Spirit of anointing, anoint them now with the love of Jesus, fill their heart with his pure love.

Where hurt, loss, rejection, abuse, etc., have resulted in a broken heart. Or even a heart impaired through illness

Dear Lord Jesus, whose heart was broken on the cross, and whose word promises to give your people a new heart. I ask you now to put a new heart within [...........] —a completely new, big, healthy heart, just as Father designed it to be, and to fill it with your love, Jesus —love that will never fail or fade or run out. This is your love just for them. Fill their heart to overflowing with your love, so that it can overflow to others without ever being diminished. Thank you Jesus.

For freedom from fears
Whether working with one person or a group the prayer minister can pray as follows.

Lord Jesus I ask you now that, through the Holy Spirit, if there is any person here who has fear in their hearts, to take them back in time and space in their heart and mind, to the time when that fear came in – when they may have been overwhelmed by the powers of darkness and fear; and I pray now that you will manifest your mighty power and bring those areas into the healing light of Jesus today. Thank you, Jesus. And in the name of Jesus I take authority over every spirit of fear, and command that you be loosed and gone from every person here now, in Jesus' holy Name. Thank you Jesus.

Cursing
—by others

Lord Jesus, you were made a curse on the cross so that man should never need to suffer under a curse. You rose from the dead so that man would be redeemed from even the ultimate curse of death, into eternal life. Through the blood you shed, you made payment in full for any curse that has been put upon this person by others. I declare such curses null and void, and tell you, Satan, that the authority you had over them through those curses has no longer any power to harm or yoke them.

—by ourselves

Father, where I have knowingly or inadvertently cursed myself, by word, action or deed or connection with anything relating to the occult, I ask your forgiveness. I repent in the name of Jesus, who was made a curse for me on the cross so that I need no longer live under a curse. Therefore, by the blood of Jesus in full reparation for my sin, I declare the curse null and void and tell you, Satan, that you no longer have any hold or authority over me through that curse. Thank you, Jesus.

Genetic disorder

Father God, by the freedom that Jesus won for me on the cross, that I need not be subject to any of the sins, genetic disorders or disabilities of my forebears, as a child of God I claim that I am free. Therefore, through your grace and mercy, Father, as Jesus bore my sins on the cross, and by his wounds I am healed, I declare full health into my body and mind, in Jesus' name. With the sword of the Spirit I cut myself free from any harmful association, and with the sword of the Spirit I also cut free and declare my children free from any generational disorder which may have come through me.

Release from generational ties

Father God, it says in your word that the sins of the fathers will be visited upon the children. However, Lord, I am born again in the name of Jesus, I am a new creation, a child of God and therefore not subject to those generational laws. The Spirit of life has set me free from the law of sin and death. If I am affected by any ancestral sins, I cut myself free from them by the blood of Jesus, through which I have been redeemed and set free. I ask you to forgive me for any sins that I have committed in relation to theirs —particularly any sins in relation to the occult or involvement in secret societies. With the sword of the Spirit I cut myself free from any ungodly connection and from any generational spirits. I am free of it all, in the name of Jesus. Thank you Father.

Release from ungodly soul ties

Father God, where there are any ungodly soul ties [with e.g. my parents, school teachers, relatives —or anyone else] whether contracted through situations of my own making or against my will, whether through situations of abuse (verbal – sexual, physical or wrong relationships or any other kind), I ask you, though your grace and mercy, to forgive me for my part, as I forgive those who perpetrated any wrong against me. I accept your forgiveness, and by the sword of the Spirit I cut myself free from these ties, in Jesus' name.

Fear of men

Father God, I come to you in Jesus' name. I pray that, through the power of the Holy Spirit, your word will be the revealed and operational truth in my innermost being. Your word says that you will never fail or forsake me. I will therefore confidently claim that – the Lord is my shield and defender – I need not fear anything in the heavens above or the earth beneath; there is nothing that man can do to me. I renounce every thought and attitude to the contrary. I call upon you, Lord Jesus, to set me free of all my fears, and in particular the fear of men —and from any spirit of the enemy oppressing me in this matter. Thank you, Jesus.

Prayer minister: 'In the name of Jesus I take all authority over any spirit of fear of man oppressing any person here, and in the authority of the name of Jesus, I command it to go now and leave them. Thank you Jesus.'

Lack of self worth

Father God, please forgive me for all the occasions when I have doubted my worth and value. I renounce such attitudes. You first loved me, and in your love for me I confirm that I both love and accept myself. My righteousness is Jesus' righteousness living in me. This is the reality. In this I understand and believe that I am precious, even in my own sight. I offer myself as a living sacrifice to God. I submit myself to the lordship of Jesus and his perfect plan and purpose for my life —for Jesus' glory. I know that I am unconditionally acceptable to God. Thank you Jesus. Praise God.

Release from vows (See *The Anointing to Heal*, chapter 8.)

Any vow, oath, covenant

Father God, please forgive me for any just vow/oath/covenant I made and did not keep. And, Lord, I acknowledge that I should not have made any make foolish vows. I repent of such actions and ask you to release me from them, with the blood of Jesus, shed on the cross for me to be accepted as full payment for these and all my sins. Thank you Jesus for loving me so much. I accept that, in the name of Jesus, through the grace and mercy of Father God, I am now released from these vows and actions. Thank you Jesus.

Vows of undying love

Father God please forgive me and release me from any vow or promise I have made to anyone that I would love them and remain with them forever and have not kept that promise.

Marriage vows

Father God I made a vow that I would love my wife/husband until death parted us. I am sorry that I/we have broken that vow. I forgive (*name of wife/husband*) for anything that they did which contributed towards the breakdown of our marriage/relationship. I forgive anyone else who was involved in the breakdown. I ask you to forgive me for anything that I did that contributed towards the breakdown and I ask you to forgive (*name of wife/husband*). I ask you to release me from my vow and accept the blood that Jesus shed for me as payment in full for all my sins.

[*If another marriage or relationship has already been entered into:* Father God, divorce may legally end a marriage but in your eyes it does not spiritually release me from my vows. Therefore I ask you to forgive me for entering into a new relationship and making another vow before the first has been paid for. I ask you to forgive me – to release me – and to bless this new union.]

In all cases

With the sword of the Spirit I now cut myself free [*ADD IF APPROPRIATE: from all the one-flesh ties and soul ties that were made with ...., etc., and*] from all ungodly vows and unfulfilled vows I have made. Father God, I thank you for releasing me by the blood of Jesus from those vows. I repent of the sin of making them, and I thank you for absolving me. He who is free in Jesus is free indeed. I ask you, Holy Spirit, to guard and protect me, especially in areas of vulnerability [*ADD IF APPROPRIATE: so that nothing in previous one-flesh partners or in anyone else with whom they may have had one-flesh relationships can have any authority in my life.*] I also cut my children free from any ungodly ties which may have come down through me or from others.

APPENDIX 1

Handout Notes for Module 1
The Nature and Will of God to Heal

What do we know of the character of God?

Ex 15:26

Ex 23:25–26

What do we know of the promises of God?

Ps 41:3

Deut 7:12–15

What did Jesus come to do?

Is 61:1

Luke 4:18–19

What did he do?

Mt 8:17

Ps 147:3

What proof did he give John?

Mt 11:5–6

What did he do for us?

1 Pt 2:24

Did Jesus have compassion and show his will?

Mt 8:1–6

Mk 1:41

Mt 9:36

Mt 20:29–34

What do the following passages show?

Acts 3:1–10

Acts 5:12–16

Mt 13:58

Are healings miracles?

APPENDIX 2
Handout Notes for Module 2
Listening to Others

Every good and perfect gift is from above, coming down from the Father of the heavenly lights, who does not change like shifting shadows. He chose to give us birth through the word of truth, that we might be a kind of firstfruits of all he created. My dear brothers, take note of this: Everyone should be quick to listen, slow to speak and slow to become angry, for man's anger does not bring about the righteous life that God desires (James 1:17–20).

Session 1
Why is it important to be a good listener?
So people know they are being 'received' or attended to.

To allow the difficulties to surface.

To allow the healing needs to be revealed.

To facilitate resolution and healing.

To enable us to be conduits through whom the Holy Spirit flows into others.

Workshop 1:   Exercise 1 in listening
– Good for short term listening
Choose a partner – someone you don't know

Give a brief description of yourself – name and a few personal details

3 mins (each)

After each has a turn, repeat to your partner what you were told.

Check with your partner on how you did

Workshop 2:   Exercise 2 in more intensive listening
Write down 15 things about yourself in 5 minutes

1	2
3	4
5	6
7	8
9	10

11   12

13   14

15

Choose a different partner.

Partner 1 shares in conversational style (referring to list when necessary). Partner 2 gives feedback on what he/she has heard.

Partner 1 Tick off how many points covered so partner cannot see. (15 minutes)

Change and repeat so Partner 2 now shares and 1 listens, etc. (5 minutes)

Session 2
What are the skills needed for listening?

Preparation
Peaceful: Relaxed – Be 'prayed up; deal with distress or disturbance before you meet up with 'client'. Make sure you have no issues with unforgiveness, unbelief, unwillingness.

Responsiveness – outward:
Expressing availability – welcoming: smile or gesture
Look interested – nodding, affirming noises e.g. 'yes', etc.
Kindness
Contact
Use of eye-to-eye contact
Speech – 'I see': 'Oh; yes'; 'Mmmm'
Physical touch – always make sure this is appropriate: some people do not want any physical contact at all. Respect this.
Asking questions to clarify or to summarise ONLY
Allowing silence

Responsiveness – inward:
Listening to and watching for touch of the Holy Spirit. or when to give any words of knowledge, etc.
Be alert to any personal issues rising up
Watchfulness

Body language: open/closed postures

Mixed signals e.g. smiling whilst recalling painful/shameful/frightening things.

Appearance – brightness: tearful: tense: heavy/depressed: unkempt; ill.

Listening or inattentive   Flow of talk – fast, slow

Communication of thoughts – muddled: clear: stilted; experiencing difficulty in sharing (could be fear, shame, embarrassment etc)

Session 3
What are the barriers to good listening?

(a) Judgementalism; moral issues: lifestyles: personality conflicts. Things on which you have a particular view might come into conflict with your client. How do you listen without colluding or being judgmental?

(b) Self-awareness – know when a personal unresolved agenda has been touched upon and how to put this on hold enables objectivity (Be careful not to bury these but to work through them at a later time.)

(c) Jumping to conclusions.

(d) Finishing off sentences; putting words into the other person's mouth – not understanding and guessing.

You should always check out where you are not sure, where something is not clear.

You should always present your conclusion as a question – checking out your understanding of what the person has said with their understanding of it.

(e) Lack of preparation   (f) Inattentiveness

(g) Overbusyness   (h) Tiredness

(i) Power/neediness issues (your own)

Allow 10 minutes for questions and comments

Suggested book list for further reading

Michael Jacobs, *Swift to Hear* (SPCK, 1985)

Joyce Huggett, *Listening to Others*

Myra Chave-Jones, *The Gift of Helping* (IVP, 1982)

Roger Hurding *Roots and Shoots* (Hodder & Stoughton, 1985)

John and Paula Sandford *The Transformation of the Inner Man* (Logos, 1982)

APPENDIX 3

Handout Notes for Module 3
Knowing our Authority in Jesus

Recap on Module 1 – **Knowing the Nature and Will of God to Heal** – *because that is paramount.*

Having established that it is God's nature and will and that it was Jesus' intention to accomplish this by his death on the cross, we look at why do we think that we should be able to continue in this work.

(1) What was the commission to the 12 and the importance of the kingdom?
Matthew 9:35

Matthew 10:1–8

Luke 9:1–6

(2) What was the commission to the 70?
Luke 10:1–29

(3) What was the commission to the disciples?
Matthew 28:17–20

(4) And what were the disciples to do?
Mark 16:15–20

(5) Discuss what the Bible means by a believer?
John 5:24

John 14:12

(6) What does Jesus say about being born again?
John 3:3

(7) Having established what a believer is, do you know that you are a Christian – that you are a believer?
What work does God ask a believer to do?
Jesus answered, "The work of God is this: to believe in the one he has sent" (John 6:29).

(8) When did Jesus start to heal?
Jesus returned to Galilee in the power of the Spirit, and news about him spread through the whole countryside (Luke 4:14).

> *"The Spirit of the Lord is on me,*
> *because he has anointed me*
> *to preach good news to the poor.*
> *He has sent me to proclaim freedom for the prisoners*
> *and recovery of sight for the blind,*
> *to release the oppressed...."*
>
> (Luke 4:18)

(9) What did Jesus promise us?
I am going to send you what my Father has promised; but stay in the city until you have been clothed with power from on high" (Luke 24:49).

At Pentecost they received that anointing in power. Can you think of other terms that are used for the anointing?

(i)
(ii)
(iii)
(iv)
(v)
(vi)
(vii)
(viii)
(ix)

(10) What does the anointing do?
In that day their burden will be lifted from your shoulders,
their yoke from your neck;
the yoke will be broken
because you have grown so fat.

(Isaiah 10:27).

Do you know you have the anointing – are you baptised in the Spirit?   Yes   No

(11) We know that Jesus came to heal – we know that Jesus healed – we know that Jesus had authority over everything
Then Jesus came to them and said, "All authority in heaven and on earth has been given to me" (Matthew 28:18).
In the commissions he gave that authority to us. Even further:
In this way, love is made complete among us so that we will have confidence on the day of judgment, because in this world we are like him (1 John 4:17).

(12) Can we expect to see healing today?
Different theologies of healing
Dispensational theology. (Luther etc.)
Experiential theology
Intervention theology
Name others
Pragmatic (George Bennet)
Holistic
Trinitarian
Sacramental, etc.

Note the difference between Intervention and Absorption theologies.
Remember the diagrams.

Intervention theology
Also when we see the different ages in the diagram we see how:

(13) In the ministry of Jesus, the kingdom of God is central
After John was put in prison, Jesus went into Galilee, proclaiming the good news of God. "The time has come," he said. "The kingdom of

God is near. Repent and believe the good news!" (Mark 1:14–15).

The healings by Jesus – 25% of Gospels is about healing

(14) What do others say about the subject of the kingdom?
Jean Darnell: Life in the overlap
Kummel disagrees —all eschatological
Schweitzer —'interim ethic'
Gustaf Aulen —"Justification is simply the atonement brought into the present so that here and now the Blessing of God prevails over the curse."
J V Taylor —"If a theology of hope means that we lose our assurance of the already givenness of the Kingdom then it is defective"
Alan Ecclestone —"The Kingdom signified a life to be laid hold of now, within the Kingdoms of the earth."
J A T Robinson —"The Koinonia or Common ownership of the Holy Spirit was the distinctive thrilling announcement of the new age with the Holy Spirit as the window into everything that God in Christ means for us."

(15) Do you know about the word and believe it?
The truth is in the word —*rhema*.
The life is in the word.
"For they are life to those who find them and health to the whole body." Read on Prov. 4:20–27
It is the word that sets us free. What does the word say? —NOT EXPERIENCE.
"Nothing is impossible to God." Do I believe that?

Yes   No

APPENDIX 4
Handout Notes for Module 4
Gifts of the Spirit

The Anointing to Heal contains many illustrations of the use and definition of the gifts of the Spirit, which can be used when teaching this module. Chapter 6 particularly focuses on the use of the prophetic gifts.

Gifts of the Spirit
Ask the delegates to take about ten minutes to write down as many answers as possible to the following questions:
—To give their definition of 'Gifts of the Spirit'
—When was the Spirit first given to the church?
—How many gifts of the Spirit can they name?
Bring them back together and in order share and discuss what they have written.
With the answers to number 3 write them up on the board.

Gifts
Name the gifts in these scriptures:

Acts 2:1–4	Romans 5:16–18	Romans 6:23
Romans 12:6-8	Eph 4:11–13	Heb 2:4
Heb13:20–21	1Cor 14:22	Eph 3:10
2Tim 1:6		

Which gifts have you...
—received?
—been given?
—how and when do you use it (them)?   Do you desire other gifts?

Gifts (spiritual)
We shall look at the gifts of the Spirit in the context of being equipped by God to minister to others where we are in our local church —in other words the Body of Christ in action.

In Ezekiel 11:19f we read of this provision — *I will give them an undivided heart and put a new spirit in them; I will remove from them their heart of stone and give them a heart of flesh. Then they will follow my decrees and be careful to keep my laws. They will be my people, and I will be their God.*

The wonderful thing about this to me is the sense of belonging: *They will be my people.* Joel 2:28f reiterates this— *"And afterward,*

I will pour out my Spirit on all people. Your sons and daughters will prophesy, your old men will dream dreams, your young men will see visions. Even on my servants, both men and women, I will pour out my Spirit in those days."

Again this sense of belonging —my Spirit on my people. Both prophets were prophesying about the Spirit of God impacting mankind with the possibility of new birth and the spiritual equipping to live in the power of the Holy Spirit being given, and we know this started at Pentecost when he did indeed come in a demonstration of presence and power and birthed the Church as described in Acts 2:1-4. *When the day of Pentecost came, they were all together in one place. Suddenly a sound like the blowing of a violent wind came from heaven and filled the whole house where they were sitting. They saw what seemed to be tongues of fire that separated and came to rest on each of them. All of them were filled with the Holy Spirit and began to speak in other tongues as the Spirit enabled them.*

Our purpose

What is the purpose of the church? *What agreement is there between the temple of God and idols? For we are the temple of the living God. As God has said: "I will live with them and walk among them, and I will be their God, and they will be my people"* (2 Cor 6:16).

What is the function of its members? First to believe in Jesus whom God sent, and through whom they have his life. *Jesus answered, "The work of God is this: to believe in the one he has sent"* (John 6:29).

Secondly, to share this good news by telling it to others and by witnessing to it through our lifestyles. *He said to them, "Go into all the world and preach the good news to all creation"* (Mark 16:15ff).

Thirdly to love and serve one another wherever and however that is necessary, through the power of the Holy Spirit and in the ways he leads us to do so. *This is my command: Love each other* (John 15:17). The ministry we have is the ministry of reconciliation. *We are therefore Christ's ambassadors, as though God were making his appeal through us. We implore you on Christ's behalf: Be reconciled to God* (2 Corinthians 5:20).

From the many gifts we unearthed earlier, we want to concentrate on what in 1 Corinthians 12 are referred to as the spiritual gifts. When we are baptised in the Holy Spirit we are filled with the Holy

Spirit. The gifts belong to the Holy Spirit. We never own these gifts, they are never our gifts. He simply enables us to move in his gifts. Therefore when we are filled with the Holy Spirit we can use all the gifts. We are all filled with the same Holy Spirit. For example, no one receives a mute Holy Spirit, therefore we can all speak in tongues. The fact that we might not have used the gift of tongues does not mean that we cannot speak in tongues but simply that we are not using the gift. Whereas in fact he wants us all to speak in tongues because tongues is the only gift which is for us, for our edification, for building us up.

We would like to consider the nine gifts listed in 1 Corinthians 12 in three groups: gifts of utterance, gifts of power, gifts of revelation. Each group contains three gifts.

Gifts of Utterance

Tongues

For anyone who speaks in a tongue does not speak to men but to God. Indeed, no one understands him; he utters mysteries with his spirit (1 Corinthians 14:2). This gift is given to an individual so that God may build us up in the life of his Spirit. Praying in tongues is what we do individually and for which no interpretation is required. Speaking in tongues is when the message is for a congregation and interpretation is required, vital in fact. So we need to be aware of the difference in praying and speaking so that we do not use the gift of tongues inappropriately.

Interpretation

Look up these verses: 1Cor 14:5, 13, 27.

As mentioned, interpretation is what is needed when someone has spoken in tongues publicly and so that all may hear, understand and be edified. The gift of interpretation is also employed in explaining dreams. In both instances we must be subject to the inspiration of the Holy Spirit. Remember: *to each one the manifestation of the Spirit is given for the common good* (1 Corinthians 12:7).

Prophecy

But everyone who prophesies speaks to men for their strengthening, encouragement and comfort (1Cor 14:3). Here we have the New Testament reason for prophesying— to edify or build up, to encourage or exhort, and to comfort.

At that moment the curtain of the temple was torn in two from top to bottom. The earth shook and the rocks split (Matthew 27:51).

We are to seek the King and the kingdom for ourselves, and not go constantly to prophetic people looking for personal words of direction. This is not to say that someone else may not have a prophetic word for us, just that we should not always be seeking others to tell us what the Lord is wanting to say to us. *"My sheep listen to my voice; I know them, and they follow me"* says Jesus in John10:27, and so we should follow him, listen to him and obey him. We should not be investing in others what really belongs to God —our trust and faith in his leading for our lives. So in praying for others we can be led by the Holy Spirit to speak words which will encourage them, build them up or comfort them. We should not sit back and say that we are not sure that we hear the Lord. Why not? Why not go after the uncertainty rather than live with it. Jesus says that we, his sheep, hear his voice. If you feel that you do not know or hear the Lord's voice – and it is just a feeling, because the truth is that you do hear it and know it – ask him to show you. Then as the good shepherd that he is he will come out and get you and show you.

Again, beware of speaking out of soulishness, wait for the Lord to formulate the words for you and then you can speak them out. Do not be so swayed by another's sorrow or agony that you rush straight into trying to fix them. That may be your anxiety, your discomfort, or may be touching on unhealed issues in your own life. Wait for the Lord. It is his words which have eternal life not ours.

2. Revelation Gifts

Word of wisdom

To one there is given through the Spirit the message of wisdom, to another the message of knowledge by means of the same Spirit (1 Cor 12:8). This is usually used to resolve difficult or apparently unanswerable situations. For instance, Jesus, when asked if he would pay taxes (which was a veiled way of saying do you support Rome or us), answered by showing a coin and asking whose head was on the coin. Upon being told Caesar's he then answered render unto Caesar the things of Caesar, but to God the things of God. *"Caesar's," they replied. Then he said to them, "Give to Caesar what is Caesar's, and to God what is God's"* (Matthew 22:21). In the Old Testament we are given a very good example of the kind of wisdom we are looking at, in the situation where Solomon gave the decision on which of the women should have the baby.

You may be told of a very difficult situation and be asked to give your opinion or solution. Beware! And be aware that this is where you need the Holy Spirit to reveal the word of wisdom appropriate to that situation. What is not needed is your opinion or your solution, or, indeed, your assessment. Don't be seduced into trying to sort it all out. Only do what the Lord shows you to do and only say what the Lord tells you to say. If he shows you nothing, then do nothing; if he tells you nothing, then say nothing.

Word of knowledge
To one there is given through the Spirit the message of wisdom, to another the message of knowledge by means of the same Spirit (1 Corinthians 12:8). These are things revealed by the Holy Spirit of which you could have no knowledge. It will speak volumes to your hearer and usually will mean little or nothing to you. Indeed this gift is sometimes very difficult to grow in as we believe that what has come into our minds is so trivial, or unrelated to what has come about, that we can dismiss it out of hand or overlook it. For instance, they may have come with a broken leg and all you have is a picture of swans landing on a lake —and that might seem a crazy thing to tell them. Remember, if you have committed yourself to serve the Lord, he will give whatever is need in that situation. He will make you aware and will give you ways of saying it. You can offer what you aware of, like this: 'I have a strong sense/a picture of/a feeling of/a place of peace or a swan gliding on a lake or whatever it is, and then say, 'Is this significant for you?' Usually it is. Remember it is in God's purposes to train and encourage us! As an example – a lady came to me with a neck and back problem but all I had was a picture in my mind of a snowy night and told her so. It turned out that it was on such a night that the neck and back problem had started. She had

received a shock when some snow fell off a roof on to her. I spoke into the trauma of that night which was still holding her in shock, and told it go and set her free. Her neck and back problem were immediately released and the pain left.

Discernment of spirits

After this, Jesus traveled about from one town and village to another, proclaiming the good news of the kingdom of God. The Twelve were with him, (Luke 8:1). *At that very time he cured many people of diseases and afflictions and evil spirits...* (Luke 7:21). This is something we can expect to come up against as we ask the Holy Spirit to lead us into the truth. If you are praying for others it is important to be well prepared, and preparation beforehand will equip you to be clear channels of this particular gifting. Be sure you are clear to pray with no unforgiveness, bitterness or outstanding agendas. Any of these things cloud our vision, and the things of darkness can hide with ease around us where we are in darkness too. So come walking in the light of God and cleared up to that point of any known sin.

Do not engage in conversation with any demonic presence that the Lord is showing you. Resist it and it will flee from you. You can pronounce cleansing prayers or words of command as the Holy Spirit directs, but definitely do not engage in conversation. Be sensitive in your use of language. The person you are praying for may be terrified at the thought of having a demon, or knowing they are around them. And I repeat, follow the leading of the Spirit in your use of language and communication of what he gives you.

3. Gifts of Power

Faith

For by the grace given me I say to every one of you: Do not think of yourself more highly than you ought, but rather think of yourself with sober judgment, in accordance with the measure of faith God has given you (Romans 12:3). Each person has a measure of faith and it is this we move in at all times because without it is impossible to please God. But this *gift* of faith is one given for specific times or occasions. With it, we can claim on behalf of the other person the provision the Lord has just shown. This gift manifests itself in an 'I know that I know that I know' type of way. The certainty not that it will be done but that it has been done is just so concrete that there are no questions in your mind or heart. It is established.

Miracles
These come along in the course of the ways of praying that we have been discussing. They are distinctive, not always instantaneous, but absolutely only in God's power to do —such as the changing of wine into water, etc.

Healings
We see a lot of these at the Centre, small and large, tender and amazing. Often used in conjunction with the other gifts mentioned before.

Life of Jesus
'For in Christ all the fullness of the Deity dwells in bodily form, and you have been given fullness in Christ' (Col 2:9). In Jesus all the 'gifts' are present. As I mentioned at the beginning, God is the Giver, and it is God we must put on and live in at all times. The gifts of the Spirit are of God. *...and above all these virtues put on love which binds them all together in perfect unity* (Col 3:14). Also, see 1 Cor 13:1. *If I speak in the tongues of men and of angels, but have not love, I am only a resounding gong or a clanging cymbal.* This is the true place of focus for us when we think of the giftings of the Holy Spirit. God is love. If we try to move in any of the gifts without him, we are told we are a resounding gong. We miss the mark.

1 Cor 12	—	Shows us the gifts of the Spirit
Eph 4	—	Shows us the gifts of the Son
Romans 12:6–8	—	Shows us the gifts of the Father

As we look at the individual 'gifts', let us not forget that this is of God. Let us learn to be able workmen with his word, and approach him with the reverence and awe which is appropriate, and 'use' his gifts with gratitude and respect.

APPENDIX 5

Handout Notes for Module 5
The Cycle of Grace

Much of the following material is taken from Learning to Listen *which is one of the many* Listening *training courses provided by the Acorn Christian Healing Foundation. For information about their training courses and resources please look them up at their website address of: www. acornchristian.org*

Divide into couples, preferably with someone who you know little about – just listen; no commenting to each other – for two minutes each. In those two minutes just say something, which you feel is relevant about yourself at this time.

Now the whole group together

Cast your mind back over the past week. Not counting this evening —who has been listened to in a way that was meaningful when you needed it? Past year? Ever?

Who has not been listened to?

How many have been listeners for someone else in the same way?

Dr Frank Lake, who founded the Clinical Theology Association (now The Bridge Pastoral Foundation) and the whole field of clinical theology. Lake (d.1982) and Emil Brunner, a Swiss theologian, were trying to find a model for people to live by through which they could live a completely balanced and resourced life. They realised that this could only be modelled on a perfect person. The only perfect man available was and is Jesus, so they examined aspects of his life and from that devised a model to work from. They called this model The Dynamic Cycle.

In some way or other we are all called into a life of service. Constantly all kinds of conflicting demands are being forced upon us. This is especially true in the lives of those who are involved in caring professions or caring roles. This must include raising families and running homes. How do we do this without constantly finding ourselves drained flat like batteries, and worn out?

They looked at Jesus in his three years of ministry. Think of all that happened in those three years —and, as we are told, just a tiny fraction of all that happened and what he did is recorded. Yet he seemed to do everything calmly and matter-of-factly with a complete sense of order and peace around him.

Think of some such events. They could include such as: when they were going to stone him, he walked quietly through their midst – or to arrest him —he stood and waited whilst they picked themselves up. On the cross he took the time to think of others, including his mother's future. From all the stories emanates a profound trust in Father.

How do we do this? See the diagram below (p171).

Acceptance

This all basically about unconditional acceptance and how we need to have this written deep, deep into our very being —just as Jesus did. *...and the Holy Spirit descended on him in bodily form like a dove. And a voice came from heaven: "You are my Son, whom I love; with you I am well pleased"* (Luke 3:22).

Do you know that you are God's beloved son and that he is well pleased with you?

You probably often pray or talk to God and tell him things. Do you expect him to hear and expect him to reply? Jesus did.

So they took away the stone. Then Jesus looked up and said, "Father, I thank you that you have heard me. 42 I knew that you always hear me, but I said this for the benefit of the people standing here, that they may believe that you sent me" (John 11:41, 42).

Jesus knew that he was not only always heard but always had been heard.

(Maybe give examples from your own life.)

Sustenance

Do you know that all that you ever need or will need to keep you sustained can and will be supplied by Father God —if we can come to a place of being totally trusting and reliant on him? To be fully human is to be fully dependent on God.

Whenever Jesus was under pressure, or had decisions to make, before he did anything he went to Father God. Before he was to make the momentous decision that was to have an everlasting effect of the world, the decision to choose the disciples, he was under attack from the Pharisees. He did not draw up a 'Disciple Profile' —he did not write a job description; he did not advertise and ask for CVs, then draw up a shortlist after interview! No, he went and spent the night with the Father and then came down and announced his decisions. He and his Father decided together. He got all the wisdom and insight that he needed.

Read Luke 6:12–16
If he needed anything – wisdom, courage, strength, discernment – he went to the Father and knew he would receive. As he said to the disciples, *"So I say to you: Ask and it will be given to you; seek and you will find; knock and the door will be opened to you"* (Luke 11:9).

Significance
Jesus had no doubts about who he was. He knew who he was. He knew who 'I am' was, and all of this flowed out from the fact that he knew he was unconditionally loved. Look up:

John 6:35
John 10:7
John 10:11
John 11:25
John 14:6
John 15:5

Do you know that this also works for you? Because...
In this way, love is made complete among us so that we will have confidence on the day of judgment, because in this world we are like him (1John 4:17).

Achievement
So many of us get completely worn out trying to prove that we are worthwhile —by all the things that we do and have done. But do we ask Father first whether he wants us to do this? Remember the work of the Father is this, that we believe that he whom he sent is the Son of God.

Jesus only did the Father's works. He told us he only did what he saw the Father do and said what he heard the Father say. Achievement for Jesus was not to do what he thought people needed or wanted of him, or what would make him popular —he only did what the Father asked. He was in total obedience.

Look at some of the things that Jesus did.

Jesus did all these things in dependence on the Father. All things flowed from the starting point of being accepted, and the achievements flowed from this, not the other way round. This is the flow of the dynamic cycle. Always refreshed, always sustained, always sure of his ground and who he was, whether they were trying to kill him or lock him up as a lunatic (remember his family wanted to do this).

Jesus' relationship with the Father through prayer was one of his resources for sustenance. We were made to be in relationship with Father in the midst of the world.

Jesus went into the hills and desert. How do you get sustained in the world? (E.g. seeing hills, flowers, snowy days, birdsong; being with friends and family, etc., as well as in times of praise, worship and ministry.)

How many of us are fully aware that in Jesus we have the opportunity to receive and know the acceptance, the sustenance, the significance of who we are —and then let the achievements flow out from this.

Instead of a dynamic cycle we tend to work in a cycle of frustration because we go the wrong way round. We are always trying to prove that we are worthwhile and worthy because of what we have done.

When someone asks whether or not you have had a good day. What do you say? 'Not very good, I did not get much done'? Or— 'Great; I managed to do so and so, and so and so....' See how so often we are more aware of what we are *doing* rather than who we are *being*. Dorothy always says that God made 'beings' not 'doings'.

Look at some of the reasons we may be blocked from fully knowing our acceptability to God:

Fear of rejection, and experiences of not being acceptable or worthwhile.

E.g. Nothing you did reached mum or dad's standards or requirements of you.

Not wanted at home.

Wallflower at a dance.

Not picked for teams: football, neball, etc.
Too fat or the wrong shape or physique for PE.
Not clever enough to pass exams.
Not able to get the job you wanted.
Passed over at work.
Made redundant.
'Big boys don't cry.'
'Now you are the man of the house.'
'All girls should be able to sew, cook, and bake.'

- **We need to flow dynamically, always knowing that we are unconditionally acceptable to God, and therefore we will be sustained in everything by him.**
- **We are significant purely and simply because he loves us and accepts us.**
- **All our achievements flow in loving obedience to him.**

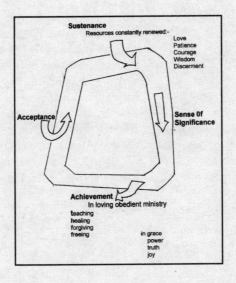

APPENDIX 6

Handout Notes for Module 6
Models of Ministry

Section 1: Models of ministry

How many ministry methods can you think of?
How many are you familiar with in using yourself?

Model	I use / don't use
laying on of hands	use

Use continuation sheet if you think of more.

Having answered this question, let's see how many different models
Jesus used.

A Touching the sick person

Mark 16:18
Mark 8:22–25

B Speaking to the sickness

Luke 4:39
John 5:8
Mark 9:25
Luke 5:19–20
Mark 10:52
John 4:46–50

C Touching the sick person and speaking to the sickness

Mark 1:41
Mark 5:41
Mark 7:33
John 9:6–8

D Sick people touching Jesus

Luke 6:19
Mark 6:56
Mark 5:28–30

E Faith and authority
Mark 11:23–24
Heb 11:1
Matt 28:18
Matt 10:1
James 5:15

F Forgiveness
Mark 11:25–26

G Distance healing
Acts 19:11–12

H Anointing
Mark 6:13
James 5:14

Section 2: Practicalities of ministering: a self assessment
Answer for yourself whether you feel you know how to work in all the following practical situations, e.g. do you know how to catch someone without doing you or them an injury? Or, do you know how to anoint with oil?

Catching
Do you know how to catch safely?

To stand or to sit
—Does it matter?

Gender to gender
Should it be same sex ministry always, sometimes, never? Remembering we are talking about an open meeting, then there really isn't a problem here. However, some people may have been abused and find difficulty with men for example, so we should not force people to have to go to any one minister – let them choose

To hug or not to hug?
Is hugging appropriate? When? When is it not? Maybe the person has been abused and the thought of being hugged by a man will have

them running away, not coming to receive ministry. Some people may find their attention drawn to the minister not to Jesus. Sometimes, people need to feel the arms of Jesus around them. If in doubt —don't, especially male to female.

But remember, we are talking about ministering in an open forum, so there is less likelihood of cries of inappropriate behaviour being made.

Touching
Should you touch or avoid touching? When is it good to touch and is it ever wrong to? Touch is good and healthy, but can be frightening for some. Touch should be gentle and light, but not so light as to be tickly. Touch should not be forceful. Smith Wigglesworth punched someone hard in the stomach who had cancer, but this would be unlawful nowadays. Don't push people over to make yourself feel successful. Offering touch when people come forward, but not requiring it, is welcoming without being threatening.

Volume and sensitivity
How loudly should you talk to the client?
—Loudly enough that they can hear clearly without straining. If they are straining, try to get it so that they aren't;
—Quietly enough so that confidentiality is maintained

Confidentiality and supervision need
Should you share the problem with another if you feel stuck, and with whom should you share? If you are stuck you could say to the person that you are going to get someone else to help pray – is that alright?

If you have a problem yourself afterwards, then take it to the person in charge of the meeting. You need to get difficulties sorted out that you have had raised in you —and those in authority for the meeting/ group, etc are there for you as much as for those coming for prayer. Do not take the details of a ministry time to anyone else —people require and deserve confidentiality.

Medication considerations and doctors
What should you do if someone asks if they should continue taking their medicine if they feel healed?

a. tell them to keep taking the medication and seek their doctor's advice.

Modesty cloths
What are they for and when do you use them?

Tears and hankies
Are you comfortable when people get upset? Does it bother you? What do you think is the best way to handle this? Why do you get upset? Is this touching on a part of your own hurt? Module 7 touches on this. Don't try to get people to stop crying. Find the hankies, and let them be free to express whatever is within. If you know they are crocodile tears designed for attention seeking, then quietly and/or in tongues, speak to the situation and tell the person to be quiet.

Should you show emotions ever when ministering?
Sometimes God seems to give us feelings – the same physical or emotional pain. The person needs to know that we are still okay, so we may start crying, but the tears should never overtake us; we should allow them but still be available for Holy Spirit to speak to and minister through us.

Anointing with oil
Do you know how to do this? Would you feel comfortable if you had to do it right now —that you would know what you are doing?

To pray or to talk
Should you always pray over the person? Or should you sometimes counsel them? Do you know how to tell the difference? Do you feel comfortable not praying? This is dealt with in *Listening to God* (5) and *Listening to Others* (4). Basically, listen to what Holy Spirit is telling you. Avoid 'nice' prayers.

Tongues or English?
Do you know which to use and when and why?
a. English if you want the person's mind to understand Tongues if you are having difficulty in hearing God. Tongues if you feel you want to speak to the condition and bypass the person's intellectual understanding.

Deliverance
Do you know how to go about this, or are you not sure? If you are not sure, then best advice is to get someone who does. Module 3 *Knowing your authority* would be a help here.

Aligning the skeleton
Do you know how to pray about leg lengthening, back straightening and so on?

Breaking curses
Do you know how to minister breaking through word curses, generational ties, ungodly soul ties? Again, best to get some training.

Allergies, fears and phobias
Do you know how to minister in these? *a.* Again, training is useful here. Basically, you are coming against soulish strongholds, or even brokenness in the spirit, and these need to be broken down.

Do you need to understand the medical condition?
Sometimes it gets in the way. It can cause doubt in your own heart.

Is it important if the person is saved or not?
Do you need to know this?
a. Of course it is important! But they do not have to be saved to be healed. Before Jesus died and rose again, people were getting healed.

Is it important that the person is baptised in the Spirit?
Do you need to know this?
a. Again, of course it is important, but again they can be healed whether or not they have already been baptised in Holy Spirit. To find release in tongues (for example), then yes, they will need to have been baptised in Holy Spirit.

'This person has so many problems, where do I start?'
How should this situation be handled?
a. One problem at a time! Remember, you are not the answer to their

problem, Jesus is. The Holy Spirit is your source of information on how to deal with the situation, not the knowledge you have amassed over the years. See, especially, Modules 5 and 7.

Personal hygiene

Is it important? Why/why not? It is very important/ We do not want anything about us getting in the way of the person to whom we are ministering. Deodorant/fresh breath/perfume/aftershave (but not so strongly that we can smell you coming fifty paces before you walk in the door – that's the opposite of the body odour problem!)

C Practical session in pairs

Leg lengthening
Anointing with oil

APPENDIX 7

Handout Notes for Module 7
Be Clear for Prayer

Effective prayer needs a Christian, the Word, the power of the Holy Spirit at work within us.

(1) If we are interceding we have to know God's conditions before we come before the throne of grace. Therefore before we start to pray we need to know that we are praying the Father's will and therefore can expect to receive the manifestation and fulfilment of our petition. With regard to the ministry of healing therefore we must be very sure we understand *The Nature and Will of God to Heal* (Module 1). Do you know any passage in the Scriptures where Jesus or a disciple prays for healing? There are none.

Prayer is to God. We speak to the situation.

If we do not know that what we want to pray for is in God's will, then ask him first —that is part of prayer. If we are still not sure then we confess it and say nothing until we are sure – or pray in tongues – this can bring revelation.

If you think that God gives you sickness, then why go to the doctor? —Surely that in itself would then be sin, to go against what you think is God's will for you?

We must be sure that we know the authority that we have in the name of our Lord Jesus Christ. (See Module 3)

Do you know that you are a born again Christian; and under the anointing (i.e. baptised in the Spirit)?

With all that girded under our loins, we can start to think about prayer.

(2) What do you think is meant by Psalm 139:23. *Search me, O God, and know my heart; test me and know my anxious thoughts.*

Petition... *Create in me a pure heart, O God, and renew a steadfast spirit within me* (Psalm 51:10).

Resolution... *But in your hearts set apart Christ as Lord* (1 Peter 3:15).

Have you any doubt? Have you any fear? Fear of anything. Doubt and fear mean that we do not trust God in these areas of our lives.

Check out your fears: water; heights; flying; poverty; spiders; men —and so on. *Ask the class to tell about and discuss theirs.*

(Use case studies to highlight fears and the healing of them.)
When we respond to what God requires of us, then we can appropriate what he desires for us.

(3) The fundamental principles

Forgiveness	Acceptance
Of our sins	Of God as he really is
Of others	Of ourselves by ourselves
Of ourselves by God	Of others

Look at what is laid up in our hearts and overflows.

(4) Examine all that might be included in Mark 11:24–26
Therefore I tell you, whatever you ask for in prayer, believe that you have received it, and it will be yours. And when you stand praying, if you hold anything against anyone, forgive him, so that your Father in heaven may forgive you your sins." But if you do not forgive, neither will the Father who is in heaven forgive your sins.

Examine all that forgiveness and unforgiveness means. Use example of marriage break up —past, present and future. Forgiveness does not mean condoning or agreeing with the actions of any who hurt or abused us. Forgiveness is not releasing them —they will still have to work those things out with Father themselves. Forgiveness is to release oneself. Unforgiveness is allowing the abuser to have control over our lives. It is like locking oneself up in solitary confinement in a high security prison cell and handing them the key. Forgiveness is to enable us to take the key back —and, with it, control over our own future.

Consider the implications of this and ask God to highlight within you any instances which need to be dealt with.

(5) Is anyone carrying any guilt?
Yes, examine ourselves: Why are we sick? Have we left any opening for Satan or sickness to come in?
Satan is the accuser of the brethren.

What we must remember:
Therefore, there is now no condemnation for those who are in Christ Jesus (Romans 8:1)

Why?

...because through Christ Jesus the law of the Spirit of life set me free from the law of sin and death (Romans 8:2);
and,
Dear friends, if our hearts do not condemn us, we have confidence before God and receive from him anything we ask, because we obey his commands and do what pleases him (1 John 3:21f).

(6) No self-justification

(7) What do we mean by negative confession?
In Numbers 14 the land is full of giants.

(8) Have you had any occult or secret society involvement?
Talk about the need for release from any occult involvement and what that might be.
Also secret societies —masons etc.
Cleansing the house or self of any artefacts.

(9) Are others more worthy or needy or have a better case to be healed than you?
FACT — God is impartial. *For God does not show favoritism* (Romans 2:11).
Then Peter began to speak: *"I now realize how true it is that God does not show favoritism"* (Acts 10:34).
...who wants all men to be saved and to come to a knowledge of the truth (1 Timothy 2:4).
"For God so loved the world that he gave his one and only Son, that whoever believes in him shall not perish but have eternal life." (John 3:16).
And we have seen and testify that the Father has sent his Son to be the Savior of the world (1 John 4:14).
It is God's nature and will to heal.

(10) Prayers

To forgive

Father God I want to totally forgive from the bottom of my heart all the people whoever did me any harm —or against whom I have resentment and bitterness. I especially name [............]. Please help me through your grace where I am still not healed and willing. In Jesus' name, I release them all. I forgive them totally from my heart.

Also, Father, I ask you to forgive me for the times I have blamed you and blamed you.

Father, where I have been in self-condemnation and blamed myself, even after asking for and receiving your forgiveness: I accept forgiveness of myself for everything for which you have already forgiven me. In Jesus' name, I receive your forgiveness for once and for all. I am free in Jesus name.

Release from occult

Father God I repent utterly of any occult involvement which I have had in my life. Forgive me - cleanse me and set me free. Thank you Jesus.

APPENDIX 8

Handout Notes for Module 8
Listening to God

Session 1

A. How can I know that God speaks?

B. How can I be sure he wants to speak to me?

C. How can I listen to him?

D. Have I been born again of the Holy Spirit into the life of Jesus?

E. How can I be sure that God will speak to *me*?

F.   Have you found these words to be true in your experience?

So they took away the stone. Then Jesus looked up and said, "Father, I thank you that you have heard me. I knew that you always hear me, but I said this for the benefit of the people standing here, that they may believe that you sent me" (John 11:41f).

Give a few examples

Session 2
A. Personal inventory

How do I hear him most easily?

When do I hear him?

Where do I hear him?

What is the most recent thing he has said?

How did I respond?

Do signs accompany me when I pray?

Which signs have I seen after I have prayed?

What is in my mind/heart as I pray for others?......

Confidence? In what or whom?

Timidity? —for what reason, and what do I do about it?

Anxiety?

B. Praying for others

C. Questions to consider
- Am I secure in knowing God speaks to me?
- Am I working under authority in praying for others? (or willing to be so)
- Am I willing to be questioned/held accountable?

Session 3   Who is called to heal the sick?
(See Mark 16:15 to 18)

A. Knowing how to pray when ministering
The best preparation is personal intimacy with God through times spent with him, through scripture reading and growing in familiarity with the ways of God and the life of Jesus. The Holy Spirit will teach us, give us revelation and release his gifts into our lives during these times of intimacy. We also grow as we meet with and are ministered to by, other Christians. When we then come to pray with others we will have a rising confidence in knowing we hear God and in applying what he shows us or tells us to do..

B. How sure am I of what I am hearing and its source —God, the devil or self?
Four crucial elements
- The habit of asking the Holy Spirit to search your heart.
- Regular reading of the Scriptures
- Study (as opposed to reading) of God's word.
- Obedience to the will of God as you fnd it and understand it.

Read Psalm 139
Being perfected
Search your heart   —cleansed
Meditation and contemplation   —nourished
Obedience   —responsiveness

Loving God is really what it is all about.
'If you love me you will keep my commandments' said Jesus.

C. Conclusion

Nobody is perfect.	But we are being perfected.
We cannot perfect ourselves.	But God can.

How to listen to the person and the Holy Spirit

Looking at any aspect of the healing ministry almost always puts us in touch with our areas of lack.

Most meals are taken in bite sizes.

It is good to vary the intake when eating

This is also true in ways of the Spirit.

Taste and see that it is good.

A time for everything (Ecclesiastes)

Do what we can and do not worry about what we cannot.

It is *his* plan – *his* power – *his* goals – *his* ways.

We just have to keep in close with him.

APPENDIX 9
Handout Notes for Module 9
Healing through Worship

At virtually every healing service, music is an integral part. So we have to ask ourselves why this is. What is so important about worship music that virtually no service, healing or otherwise, seems to be possible without it? What part does it play for the minister and for the one receiving ministry?

1. Worship   Focussing on God, not on self
Get them to look up   Matt 16:24–27   Rom 12:1–2

I mention this at the outset, because it is absolutely prime to everything we are going to consider. Worship is what we are about. Worship is what God put us here for and it is integral to our very nature. The big sin that started off all the problems in the first place was that Satan wanted to be worshipped. That is a big all time no no. So, as we start a module on worship in healing let us set out very clearly for ourselves that none of what we do is for us. None of it is for the people who come for ministry. It's all, 100%, completely, for God. If we notice any sense of wanting to be noticed ourselves – for how hard we've worked, or how many people got really blessed or anything else in that line that you can think of – then we need to confess to God that we're sorry we've moved our focus away from him for a little, and then get focussed right back in on God. We worship him and we look for no commendation in so doing: this is all about giving all our focus and all our attention, to God. And that is worship

Temple worship
There are many types in the OT. Types are those things which were true for the day but were foreshadows of things that would come later in the Christian era as well, in a different form but with the same flavour or underlying principles. For example, the near sacrifice of Isaac by Abraham was both an actual event and also a type, foreshadowing what God the Father was doing in sending God the Son. The temple is another type. It was a style of worship for the Jews in the days of King Solomon right down to the days of Jesus and it also foreshadowed Christian worship. So, a quick look at temple worship.

The glory of the temple

King David wanted to build God a permanent house as he had one but God still lived in his tent. God said to David that Solomon would build the temple — 1 Chron 22:8. So David decided to lay up the treasure for it.

a. 1 Chron 22:5 — David wanted the whole thing to be 'forget the budget' big!

b. v 14 silver and gold = £65b plus immeasurable other stuff.

1 Chron 29:1–4 David gave c. £1.6b from his own bank account.

2. The music of the temple
prophetic

a. 1 Chron 25:1–2 prophets as ordered by the King

b. v 3 prophets who give thanks to God

c. v 5 prophets (seers) who exalt God's horn.

ordered

1 Chron 23:5 4000 worship singers

v7–8   288 skilled musicians

v 8 divided into a rota

c. 24 rota slots cf. 24:3, 19

Specific worship roles were assigned each person 1 Chron 15:16–21

Points to note

The temple was lavish. God wanted it to be an awesome place that people came into to worship him. If you do a study on the tabernacle, you will see that it too was a truly outstanding and awesome tent.

God expects praise & worship 24/7 from his congregations and puts worship leaders within the body to enable worship. There was always worship in the temple, whether there was a service going on or not!

There is nothing slapdash about the way GOD wants worship conducted. He had 24 hour a day, professional musicians conducting worship in his temple (1 Chron 9:33 and 16:41). So why should we be any different?

It was the Levites, not the priests, who offered worship. That is, the laity.

Now go to Matt 27:51 where the veil is torn asunder and so all God's people can now come into intimate close communion with God.

3. Worship in heaven

(a) Isa 6:1–4
- Smoke filled, like the incense filled temple
- God sitting enthroned like in the Holy of Holies
- Continual praises being sung

(b) Rev 4:7–11

(c) Rev 7:9–17

(d) Rev 8:1–6

(e) Rev 11:15–19

(f) Rev 14:1–5

(g) Rev 15:1–4

(h) Rev 19:1–10

Special notes from (h)

4. Praise or worship —both defined biblically

It may surprise you to know this, but praise and worship in the Bible are not the same thing. There are many words for praise in the OT, and we will look at some of them; there is one word only in each of the OT and NT for worship.

(a) Praise words

HALAL
= to praise Yahweh = to praise God.
Has sense of boastful, excited, to enjoy. Cf. David dancing before the ark and his wife Michal being offended by his cavorting.

YADAH
Ps 138:1 = public acknowledgement
Exciting throwing up of arms. Cf. 2 Chron 20

BARAK
To bless
Ps 103:1–2 Bless the Lord, O my soul
Sense of kneeling and bowing

ZAMAR
Music making to God
=to touch the strings
Ps 150
SHABACH
Ps 117:1
To laud, speak well of
To address loudly, to shout, to glory
TOWDAH
Thanksgiving for past and future help
Therefore an act of faith
Praise now for salvation later
TEHILLAH
To sing, to laud
Singing halals
Ps 22:3 & 2 Chron 20:22
Unprepared singing = singing in the spirit
RUAH
To shout in joy
Ps 95:1 and 100:1
QARA
Proclamation
Ps 116:17
NAGAD = to declare Ps 9:11b
BASAR = to proclaim
RUM = to extol

(b) Worship words

OT is in Hebrew, and the word is *shachah.* This occurs 172 times, 2 of which mean to crouch (1 Sam 2:36) or to stoop (Prov 12:25). The other 170 mean to worship, to bow down, to do obeisance, to reverence, to fall down (before).

NT is in Greek and the word is *proskuneo.* All 60 occasions are translated as worship. Both of these have the idea of deferring to one greater than yourself. They incorporate the action of bowing down before in homage. To worship then, is to give the place of honour and esteem to another in both words and action. There is no place for self— self-consciousness, self-centredness, self-acknowledgement, etc. All our attention and thoughts and feelings are focussed on acknowledging the one who is the object of our worship.

5. Conclusions so far

Worship is what we are about

God has ordained worship as an integral and important part of our life

Worship goes on in heaven

Worship is often (more often than not) noisy

Worship involves the whole person

Praising God can lead to intense worship, e.g. Rev 19

Worship is to be lavish

Worship should be wholehearted and fully entered into

Worship has a physical effect – thunderings in heaven: physical well being brought on through exercise

6. Effects of praise and worship

(a) Josh 6:1–21

(b) 1 Chron 20

(c) Acts 2:42–47

(d) Acts 3:1–9

(e) Acts 3:11–4:4

(f) Acts 4:23–31

(g) Acts 16:24–26

(h) 1 Sam 16:22–23
Anointed playing brings healing

(i) Ex 17:8–13

7. The power of agreement in praise and worship

(a) Ps 22:3 *But You are holy, Enthroned in the praises of Israel.*

(b) 'When praise and worship is loosed by a group, there is a tremendous amount of power generated. Ps 22:3 says that God inhabits the praises of his people. When we praise God together, God inhabits our praise. Because corporate praise involves the power of agreement, the power of coming into harmony, there is a tremendous spiritual energy generated.' (Terry Law, *The Power of Praise and Worship.*)

(c) Acts 4:32–37
- **Held all things in common**
- **Power accompanied the apostles' preaching**
- **None lacked**

(d) Acts 5:12–16
- **They met in the temple**
- **They were in one accord**
- **Believers added daily**
- **All that came were healed**

Many signs and wonders were done among the people, including the sick in the street healed as Peter's shadow fell on them.

(e) Matt 18:19–20 and,

(f) *The weapons we fight with are not the weapons of the world. On the contrary, they have divine power to demolish strongholds* (2 Cor 10:4).

(g) Praising is important to us as eating and breathing.

(h) Jesus prayed and then healed. (See John 11:41ff).

Question

Is there something going on in heaven between and praise happening and signs and wonders bringing victory in all facets of life? Yes!

Conclusions
- **God is present when we come together.**
- **Praise and worship brings us together in one accord.**
- **Setting our activity into praise and worship puts us in a place to receive.**
- **God will perform signs and wonders when we praise his name.**
- **We should expect the unexpected when we enter into praise and worship.**
- **The supernatural will become the norm if we dedicate ourselves to worship.**

9. Practical A few songs from the hymnody of the group should be chosen for half an hour's worship.